W9-CJX-839

COLLECTING POSTCARDS
In Colour

Frank Staff Collection

CARTOMANIAC

Collecting Postcards In Colour

1894–1914

BY WILLIAM DÛVAL
WITH
VALERIE MONAHAN

BLANDFORD PRESS
Poole · Dorset

First published in 1978
by Blandford Press Ltd,
Link House, West Street, Poole,
Dorset BH15 1LL

Copyright © Blandford Press 1978

ISBN 0 7137 0823 9

All rights reserved. No part of this book may be reproduced or transmitted in any form or by any means, electronic or mechanical, including photocopying, recording or by any information storage and retrieval system, without permission in writing from the Publisher.

Colour printed by Jarrold & Sons Ltd, Norwich
Text printed and books bound by
Butler & Tanner Ltd
Frome, Somerset, and London

Contents

5

Acknowledgements

The authors are greatly indebted to many people for their help and encouragement, and especially do we thank Messrs Raphael Tuck & Sons Ltd for their permission to reproduce postcards and advertising material published by them; the Directors and Staff of R. C. Alcock Ltd, of Cheltenham, and Mr C. W. E. Coles, of Birmingham, for providing the illustrations of postmarks; and Mrs Sally Carver for information on the American postcard market. For their practical advice and generous help, we are immensely grateful to Mr A. J. Butland, Mr Stanley Cohen, Messrs John Hall and David MacWilliams, Mr Maurice Hewlett, Mr Peter N. Lawrence, Mr Frank Staff, Mr Tony Warr and Mr Solomon L. Gluck of New York.

William Dûval
Valerie Monahan
1978

Publisher's Note

All the addresses given in this book have been carefully checked at the time of going to press and neither the publisher nor the authors can accept responsibility for any addresses which have subsequently changed. If any difficulties should arise in this connexion, please write to Valerie Monahan, P.O. Box 7, Ludlow, Salop, England.

Introduction

In 1903, someone signing himself 'A Specialist' wrote a peevish piece for *The Stamp Collectors' Fortnightly*. He was annoyed by the requests he constantly received from people he neither knew nor wished to know to exchange picture postcards with them. But the real purpose for his outburst was to define a clear distinction between, in his view, the frivolity of collecting picture postcards and the more sober pursuit of being a postcard collector. To him, the only postcards worthy of the name were those issued by the Post Office, and anything which distracted from their stark utility was anathema, so he did not mince words when he said:

> 'When one collects, as I do, real postcards (or more correctly 'postal' cards) one does not like being confused or confounded with picture-gatherers. I have nothing to say against picture cards, they are very pretty, and as souvenirs they are very interesting. But all the same I do not wish my favourite hobby, my particular study, to be compared to the more trivial pastime of picture card collecting. A postcard to my mind implies a card issued by the Post Office, and to apply this to pieces of card issued by a lithographer is clearly a misnomer. But it is, of course, too much to hope that picture card collectors will admit this, and most Post Card collectors must therefore put up with the confusion until the picture craze passes away into oblivion. ...'

A forlorn hope. Postal historians had to put up with the despised 'picture-gatherers' confusing their 'particular studies' right up until the end of the First World War. By then a legion of lives had been lost, and the postcards which had boosted the morale of both the men in the trenches and their families at home now served as poignant reminders of those who did not return. The craze for collecting postcards had been dimmed.

But despite the sadness, and the doubling of the postage rate for sending postcards to 1d, manufacturers managed to restore some of the old magic for collecting their products. Although not as splendid as the postcards published before 1914 when inks from Germany were in plentiful supply, the production of holiday views and comics continued to attract the eye until the beginning of the Second World War when a severe paper shortage forced the output of postcards to dwindle.

After the end of this war, people were too busy repairing the devastation of their towns and cities to bother about any of their pre-war activities. Besides, a whole new world of technological wonders was starting to unfold in which there would be neither the room nor the time for viewing old postcards. With energetic despatch, boxes, cartons, and albums were hustled off to the junk shops and jumble sales, or banished by the more prudent to dust-collecting attics. Tables, thus cleared of obsolete clutter, were now ready to welcome the latest picture-viewing craze, the television set.

At last, it seemed, the hopes of the anonymous 'specialist' were to be truly realized. The picture-gathering interference was dead, long live postcard collectors! Picture cards had now found their true level, belonging as they did in the lowliest archives of postal history, dismissed as nothing more than convenient forms of communication with unnecessary embellishment. The evidence that these 'conveniences' could still be purchased on the basis of 'penny plain, twopence coloured' was quite irrelevant. The urge for collecting them had been quelled, and respectability restored to the search for what was postally interesting and hopefully uncommon.

But like the underground movements of the 1940–1945 war years, there were still to be found groups of determined 'picture-gatherers' dedicated to the task of preserving, if not reviving, the remains of the only hobby to have caught the imaginations of rich and poor alike on a wide international scale. Their claim was that picture postcards had earned an indisputable place in the records for posterity which would eclipse the insults they had suffered at the hands of the 'bigots' of postal history.

During those post-war years, the devoted few made regular pilgrimages to junk dealers, jumble sales, and old book shops in their quest for discarded albums and the boxes of postcards which had been thrown out by a fickle public. Dustmen were persuaded to rescue similar abandoned treasure, and charitable organizations with a willing eye for ready cash, were always prepared to part with any cards offered to them in response to fund-raising appeals.

Then in 1958, came the glimmer of light which was to spark off a world-wide recovery of the whim for collecting picture postcards. At their stamp shop in Teddington, Middlesex, Messrs Edward Westwood and A. James Butland were told that a batch of old cards was on its way. This not especially rousing piece of information was put aside and forgotten until they received a message from the local railway station to say that a number of tea-chests had arrived for their collection. Intrigued, they borrowed a van and went to pick them up. In the goods yard they found five chests, each one crammed full of postcards, over 70,000 of the things, they thought. The original owner was surprised even to have been offered £5 a chest for what he considered to be nothing but a load of rubbish which would have ended up on his garden bonfire had it been returned.

It soon became plain to Edward Westwood and Jimmy Butland that their haul was worth researching, and for the next two years they spent one day every week at the British Museum reading every book, magazine, and article to have been published on the subject of picture postcards. So intense did their enthusiasm become for a hobby which had been dormant for so long that they wanted to share their new found knowledge, and so they published the book, *Picture Postcards and All About Them*. This was followed by the institution of their research bureau for collectors, and the creation of their magazine, *The Postcard Collectors' Guide and News*.

Slowly the happy breed of picture postcard collectors began to reunite, and a new style of collecting was born. The hunt was on, the fashion set, and the field wide open for gathering in any picture postcard published prior to 1920. In 1961, Mrs Drene Brennan started the Postcard Club of Great Britain, and similar clubs were founded in America. Mr Frank Staff, one of Britain's leading postal historians wrote the excellent book, *The Picture Postcard and its Origins* published by Lutterworth Press in 1966. Two years later, Mr John Smith produced the first postal sales lists of picture postcards under the banner of the International Postcard Market. In 1971, the first priced catalogue of 'Pictorial Postcards and Postmarks' was compiled by another great British postal historian, Mr Maurice R. Hewlett, entitled 'Picton's Postcard Priced Catalogue'. And in September 1974 the co-author of this book, Mrs Valerie Monahan, founded and published the first glossy magazine, *Postcard Collectors' Gazette*, a well-informed journal for collectors by collectors for their enjoyment and furtherance of the hobby.

But despite these efforts, as far as the general public was concerned, the rediscovered charms of collecting picture postcards remained a 'closed shop' until the end of 1970 when the Victoria & Albert Museum staged a travelling exhibition to commemorate the 'Centenary of Postcards'. By this time, many of the world's great towns and cities had been given face-lifts – not always for the better – and the displays on postcards of old buildings and places no longer in existence brought pangs of nostalgia to those old enough to remember 'the good old days' when people lived in houses with space where children could safely play, and surrounded by neighbours who had time to spare for a chat and who were always on call whatever the emergency.

By the close of this exhibition in 1973 the interest in collecting old postcards had multiplied, not only in Great Britain but in

Europe and the United States of America as well. Localized post-card clubs were formed, sales fairs and bourses were organized, and specialist dealers in postcards were recognized.

Now as we approach the end of the twentieth century, the craze which captivated millions at the beginning of it holds a new generation in its thrall. The only differences are that postal historians have discovered that the picture side of postcards is often more of a help than a hindrance to their 'particular studies' of their favourite hobby, and picture postcard collectors do not go in for collecting postcards as casually as did their predecessors, for the 'new' albums follow very clearly defined themes, none of which can be dismissed as merely 'pretty' or fleetingly interesting souvenirs of the past.

So what is it that is so magical about collecting pieces of paste-board with pictures on their fronts? Countless people from all over the world have already discovered the answer – we hope that the enchantment of collecting picture postcards will be revealed in this book to countless more.

1   *The Birth of Postcards*

Long before the arrival of the first picture postcards a vogue had been set for pictorial printing. In the eighteenth century, charmingly decorated visiting cards were exchanged, beautifully embossed and embellished writing paper appeared, ornately adorned bills were proffered by tradesmen, and a great variety of trade cards were distributed by the astute business houses of the day.

But like most of the inventive ideas of that age, pictorial print was intended only for those who could indulge a fancy for whatever novelty was devised to please and tempt them. The fads and fashions of the rich and privileged were not only beyond the scope of the pockets of ordinary people, but usually of little appeal to their tastes. Visiting cards, plain, embossed, or with engraved pictures were small conceits reserved for those who considered formal introductions to be strictly social necessities. And while intricately embellished stationery provided a pleasing background for elegant handwriting, it was of no interest to the majority of people who were unable to read – let alone write.

This state of illiteracy was generally taken for granted until the institution of the Factory Act in 1802 compelled the owners of new factories to arrange for children to be taught the 'three R's'. So by the time Sir Rowland Hill had freed his scheme for a penny postage rate from the fetters of Post Office red tape in January 1840 a new generation of ordinary men and women were able to take advantage of the innovation of writing and posting letters to their relatives and friends.

The first day of issue of the new penny postage duty was on 1 May 1840, the day when the British public saw for the first time the new envelopes designed for the purpose by William Mulready. A design which was ferociously criticized for its fussy incorporation of too much symbolic detail. Even so, despite the public derision of this first envelope which represented the first pre-paid penny postage rate, it could be genuinely considered to be a fore-runner of the picture postcard.

After the establishment of the revolutionary penny post, it took no time at all for the commercial potential of pictorial print to be seen by Victorian publishers. Fine engravings of country houses, cosy scenes of domestic bliss, views of pastoral serenity, and an abundance of robust seaside humour complete with sly or bawdy captions soon began to emerge on writing paper and envelopes. Greetings cards for all conventionally happy occasions were introduced in a great variety of shapes and sizes. But the days were still far off when the simplicity of the picture postcard was to capture the imagination of the world – although many ideas for such a device had been considered, lengthily discussed, and finally dismissed as impractical. And it was not until October 1869 when Dr Emmanuel Herrman, a professor at the Wiener Neustadt Military Academy succeeded in persuading the Austrian Postal Authority to accept his invention of the first Official postcards.

A year later, on 1 October 1870, the Swiss and British Post Offices introduced their first Official cards, the date coinciding with the first day of issue of the halfpenny postage stamp in Britain. And in Britain, these thin pieces of buff card with the imprinted violet-coloured stamps were immediately popular with the British public – if not with the stationers who loudly protested against the injustice of the price of the cards being inclusive with the price of the stamp. Their argument was that for ordinary letters the cost of the stamp was extra to the writing paper and envelopes purchased from them, and the competition of the Post

Office supplying what must be considered a free gift of writing material was grossly unfair. (And it took two years before the Post Office conceded that the stationers had a point, and even then the concession amounted only to an extra halfpenny being charged for a packet of twelve of their Official postcards.) But also in 1870, in the little village of Sillé-le-Guillaume near Le Mans, France, a French stationer by the name of M. Leon Bésnardeau was occupying himself on the more interesting enterprise of producing special postcards for the use of the troops stationed at the neighbouring village of Conlie during the Franco-Prussian War. Illustrated as they were with military and patriotic designs, these were the first pictorial cards to be published. Exactly forty years later, M. Bésnardeau staked his right to claim distinction for the French as the originator of the picture postcard. The occasion he chose was his eightieth birthday when he recorded his claim on a card addressed to Madame G. Caymans, the editor of the magazines, *The Interesting Cartophile* and *The Free Exchange* at Lierneux, Belgium. This postcard, dated 1910, is now in the collection of Mr Maurice R. Hewlett, and was reproduced in the November 1975 edition of the *Postcard Collectors' Gazette*. As it turned out, perhaps M. Bésnardeau was right, for it was certainly the French who published the first pictorial postcards to be generally recognized as such – even though the world had to wait almost another twenty years for them to appear!

At the Paris Exhibition in June 1889 France celebrated the first public opening of the Eiffel Tower by producing a pictorial vignette of her magnificent new landmark on the message side of a postcard. These cards could be purchased, stamped, and posted by the visiting public from the summit of the 984-ft-high edifice. Two years later, Britain followed suit by issuing a drawing of the Eddystone lighthouse on the reverse side of an Official postcard for the Royal Naval Exhibition. Then, in 1892, Germany developed her remarkable photo-litho printing techniques which instantly attracted healthy export markets for the beautifully designed and printed picture postcards she produced.

The opening of the World's Columbian Exposition in Chicago

on 1 May 1893 was the chosen event for the début of the first American picture postcards. In units of two at a time, the public could purchase ten different aspects of the Exposition from conveniently placed vending machines for the price of five cents a time. But the United States had already recorded another claim to fame in the postcard field, for it was in 1861 that John Charlton of Philadelphia produced the idea for the first private mailing cards, the copyright for which he later transferred to a fellow Philadelphian, H. Lipman. The 'Lipman's Postal Cards', as they became known, were plainly intended for brief messages only, since the inscription and discreetly decorative borders were their sole adornment. Despite all this activity, almost another decade was to pass before the novelty of actually collecting picture postcards was to show the unmistakable signs of becoming a classless craze, and the industry of producing them into a profitable business.

Life for British publishers was far from easy, for while the Post Office had conceded that privately printed postcards could be posted with halfpenny adhesive stamps from September 1894, it refused to budge when it was suggested that the regulations governing the size of British postcards should be relaxed. It was insisted that privately produced cards had to conform to the same dimensions as the Official postcards, and it appeared of no consequence to the British Postal Authority that continental publishers were allowed to profit by the use of the standard size of postcard decreed by the Postal Union. So Germany, with her highly sophisticated printing skills, and many of her European neighbours made much of the running during the last six years of the nineteenth century.

The controversial difference in size was nothing more than an extra inch being added to the length of postcards. But that precious inch allowed the Europeans to print better and more detailed pictures on the fronts of their postcards than their British competitors were permitted to do. It also meant that there was more room for messages to be written since the picture side was the only place where they were tolerated. Figures 1 and 2 give a fair comparison of the contrast between the spaciousness of the 'Grüss vom Semmering' card which is postmarked 1896, and the cramped proportions of the British court card posted in 1899 from Newport, Isle-of-Wight. British manufacturers were obliged to make the best of the confined space of the $4\frac{1}{2}$ in. $\times$ $3\frac{1}{2}$ in. (115 mm. $\times$ 89 mm.) available to them on the court-sized cards until the Post Office finally agreed to alter the regulation regarding size.

Figures
1 and 2

Mr Adolph Tuck, managing director of Messrs Raphael Tuck & Sons, was chiefly responsible for persuading the British Postal Authority to relax the rule which had prevented Britain from entering the much more competitive field of producing privately printed postcards. And for ultimately winning the day, Mr Tuck had as his reward the advance knowledge of the date when the standard size of $5\frac{1}{2}$ in. $\times 3\frac{1}{2}$ in. (140 mm. $\times$ 89 mm.) postcards could officially be sold in British shops. On that date, 1 November 1899, Tuck's cards were the first to be seen vaunting that vital extra inch!

With the flair long associated with the firm which already held the Royal Warrant as purveyors of fine greetings cards to Queen Victoria, Messrs Raphael Tuck & Sons had officially entered the picture postcard market. From their home base at Moorfields, London, and their premises in Fifth Avenue, New York, Tuck's commissioned innumerable artists to design sets of postcards which would be of instant appeal to their customers on both sides of the Atlantic. It must not, however, be thought that Raphael Tuck & Sons was the only British firm to deserve notice. While Mr Adolph Tuck had been leading the campaigns to induce the Post Office to adopt a more liberal attitude to the requirements of British postcard manufacturers, other British publishers had been experimenting with the collotype process of printing invented by Germany. And during the years between 1894 and 1899, despite the restrictions of size, many fine picture postcards were produced in Britain.

George Stewart of Edinburgh was the first publisher to take advantage of the Post Office regulation which allowed privately printed postcards to be posted at the halfpenny stamp rate in 1894, by producing tiny views of Edinburgh on the message side of the card. In 1895, James Valentine & Sons of Dundee began to produce a wider selection of views using the collotype method of printing. The Scots were soon joined by the London house of Blum & Degen who published distinctive vignettes of urban views printed on blue card. Close on their heels, in 1896, another London firm, the Pictorial Stationery Co., introduced a number of notable picture postcards, and later produced hundreds of very fine views in their 'Peacock' series. And in the following year George Stewart of Edinburgh began to woo British imaginations with postcards featuring topical events, thus following a fashion which had already been in vogue on the continent for a number of years.

All the prominent happenings of the times were perpetuated on picture postcards, the comings and goings of Royalty attracting much of the interest. Birthdays, weddings, and deaths of anyone in the public eye were also firm favourites, and few collections were without at least one example of a postcard commemorating Queen Victoria's Diamond Jubilee in 1897.

By November 1899, the beginning of the picture postcard era had arrived – although albums were not yet to be seen on the tables of back-street parlours. In those early days, actually collecting picture postcards was merely an amusement for the avant garde who found the pictures interesting enough to be worth preserving. Understandably so, since all the pioneer picture postcards reflected the taste and discernment of the influential and much-travelled sections of world society. How could they fail to appreciate the delicacy and beauty of the early vignettes of fashionable scenes; the charm of the German 'Grüss aus' postcards with their miniature views framed with borders of intricate scrolls and squirls and floral decorations; the excitement of the first Art Nouveau cards by artists such as Alphonse Mucha, Henri Meunier, Brunelleschi, and Arpad Basch; the breathtaking portrayals of Boer War military themes drawn by Richard Caton Woodville and Harry Payne? Even the anti-British Boer War propaganda cartoons were so well executed they were irresistible. Controversial themes were also well covered by photographers and publishers who began to see the picture postcard as a news medium. The re-trial of the French soldier Alfred Dreyfus in 1899 provided enough drama to warrant a number of scenes from the trial to appear on postcards, and there is in existence an earlier card, dated 1898 which shows four photographs of the chief characters involved in the case: Dreyfus, Esterhazy, Zola, and Labori – a card which must now be considered particularly rare.

Very few of these treasures, however, came the way of ordinary folk – unless they happened to work for the more considerate employers who frequently sent cards from abroad to their servants at home. Perhaps it was this thoughtfulness that eventually brought the pleasures of collecting picture postcards to the notice of ordinary people. On the other hand, when publishers had been given the freedom to spread their pictures over the fronts of the larger-sized postcards in November 1899, the immense commercial potential of catering for a massive public appetite was immediately seen. By 1902, the universal craze for collecting picture postcards had begun to rage like a forest fire; in fact homes without postcard albums to view were as incomplete as those without television sets today.

It was also in 1902 when F. Hartmann succeeded in getting his postcards with the divided backs off the ground. Before this, it was not permissible to write anything on the address side of a postcard other than the name and direction of the person to whom it was to be sent. But when F. Hartmann left Germany at the turn of the century to set up a postcard publishing business in Britain, he was determined to persuade the British Post Office to favour his ideas for a postcard which would allow messages to be included on the address side too, and he was rewarded by the institution of his postcards with a clearly defined line running down the middle to divide the address from the message. The contrast between the old and the new systems is shown in Figures 3 and 4 by illustrating an early St Helena Post Card with the undivided back of well before 1902 and a pictorial postcard which defines the two instructions, 'This space may be used for communications to any place in the United Kingdom' on the left hand side, and on the other, 'The address ONLY to be written here'. The choice of the St Helena card is merely to show that the regulations concerning the use of the undivided back were universal up until 1902.

This innovation, of course, gave publishers of picture postcards an even wider scope. From then on there was a pictorial commentary on every possible subject and aspect of how life was lived in the early part of the twentieth century. The comedy and the tragedy, the pomp and pageantry of great occasions, the costumes and customs of a multitude of nations, the hilarity of the music-hall and the spell-binding atmosphere of the theatre, the boats and trains and the new-fangled flying machines, exhibitions and all the fun of the fair, sporting events of every kind – and such an

PICTORIAL POST CARD.

THE ADDRESS TO BE WRITTEN ON THIS SIDE

THIS SPACE MAY BE USED FOR COMMUNICATIONS
TO ANY PLACE IN THE UNITED KINGDOM
(See Postal Regulation)

THE ADDRESS ONLY TO BE
WRITTEN HERE.

AFFIX
HALFPENNY
STAMP.

UNION POSTALE UNIVERSELLE
ST. HELENA
POST CARD
THE ADDRESS ONLY TO BE WRITTEN ON THIS SIDE.

Figures 3 and 4

endless variety of views, it seems that no place went unrecorded on a picture postcard.

And so began the first classless craze to sweep the world, for the enthusiasm for collecting picture postcards was whole-heartedly shared by everyone – no matter who they were or whether they lived in cottage or castle, the magic of the postcard album reigned supreme.

2

Topography

Travel for most people who lived in the late Victorian and early Edwardian periods was confined to a ride on a horse-drawn bus, or if they dwelt in one of the more go-ahead cities, a trip on one of the new electrified tram-cars. To the majority of the 'labouring classes', as ordinary people were described, the names of far away places were synonymous with dull geography lessons, trivia in their minds to be forgotten as speedily as possible, since it was unlikely that there would be the remotest chance that any of these foreign parts would be visited by them. So to people who never ventured much beyond the borders of their own surroundings, a picture postcard showing a portion of Brighton beach was no less a novelty than one with a view of the Eiffel Tower.

But with the arrival of picture postcard views and the subsequent craze for collecting them came a new stimulus, and a vivid splash of colour to brighten dull existences. For the price of a penny, and sometimes less, a glittering panorama of unfamiliar sights stretched out to enchant and enlighten a travel starved public. Suddenly, the whole world came alive – and very much smaller. In fact, it could be said that via the picture postcard the emancipation of the ordinary people had begun.

In those days, instant news and views on television, instant travel and tourism, instant communication and criticism, were undreamed-of marvels – or vices – of the future. But at that time it was sufficient to be able to send and receive the new pictorial postcards; to see a view of the High Street where Auntie Annie did her shopping; the stretch of seaside front where Uncle Albert sold cockles and mussels, whelks and winkles; a picture of the church where Cousin Rose was married, or the rare arrival of a card from some distant foreign land.

All over the world the public appetite for view cards soon became insatiable. Early postcard catalogues reveal that views of most countries could be bought by the dozen for as little as 1s 3d in English money, although it is interesting to note that some of the more exotic scenes were more costly. For example, there were some special scenes of Athens, China, India, and Japan on offer for 3d each – and 3d in those days was not an inconsiderable amount to pay for a postcard. And for those who cared for the niceties of having their postcards gilt-edged there were some very fine Swiss and Scandinavian studies to be had for the very high price of 4d a card! And so from the ancient mysteries of Greece, China, Egypt, and India to the younger civilizations of Europe, Great Britain, and the United States of America, the picture postcard was the first visual transmission of cultures and customs to be seen and understood by those who were not indigenous to the lands they portrayed.

Everything, no matter how small or paltry the detail, appeared on postcards. Photographers were employed on an immense scale to ensure that the phenomenal thirst for viewing how the other half lived was quenched by snapping all and anything which would be of pictorial interest. And a cursory glance through the stock of topographical cards held by most of the present-day dealers in early picture postcards will expose the difference between those photographers who accepted the challenge of the more adventurous approach of producing the 'off beat' of the day, and those who appeared to have permanent pitches for supporting their tripods and cameras at every beauty spot and popular resort imaginable.

Scenic artists were kept equally busy setting up their easels to describe in oil-paint or watercolour their versions of Edwardian life. Most of these examples are inanimate views of serenity unmarred by the hurly-burly of human intrusion, although it is not too out-of-the-way to see the occasional sketch of polite society going about whatever lawful business would gracefully suit the scene.

It was not long before a flourishing international trade in picture postcards brought a galaxy of views with unpronounceable names into every place where postcards could be purchased. And in those Edwardian days it did not matter that a view on a piece of pasteboard would be the nearest that most people would get to seeing the Niagara Falls, the Taj Mahal, the towns and cities of European countries and of the United States of America. The picture postcard had worked a small miracle, for no longer were the sights of the world the preserve of those who had the means to globe-trot whenever the fancy took them.

Perhaps, then, it is not too whimsical a presumption to claim that the picture postcard was the first medium to advance the idea that to travel the world need not be an ambition beyond the reach of ordinary men and women; maybe the fad for collecting enticing views of foreign lands acted as the spur to make the poorly paid majority look with a different eye at the boats, and trains, and the new-fangled motor-cars. Who knows what wistful dreams and aspirations flitted through the minds of those early collectors as they slotted each new treasure into their postcard albums? Fantasies which could not go further than the thought that one day their children – or at any rate their grand-children – might have the chance to travel and explore the world.

Now, of course, those dreams for an 'enlightened future' have been more than realized, but, such is the perversity of man, he is never satisfied! While the aids of modern technology and travel were denied to his Edwardian fore-fathers, *he* has become disenchanted with the plastic world of man-made this and reconstituted that transported from one place to another by aircraft travelling faster than the speed of sound. To him, the unadventurous prospect of his computerized life being determined from the cradle to the grave has, at last, made him question the reasons for his existence. The current dreams of wistfulness are shrouded with misty hankerings after anything which will give a little nostalgic diversion to the relentless treadmill of modern routine.

No wonder, then, that a new craze for collecting picture postcards has been born, for in no other field can there be captured so accurate a reflection of the life and times of bye-gone days. And so the views of yesterday are now avidly sought by the new breed of postcard collectors.

The choice is wide, for most postcard dealers hold comprehensive stocks of early view cards – or topographical as they are now called – all of which have been painstakingly classified. British views are usually sorted into counties; American scenes into States; and a good selection of countries can usually be found in alphabetical order. Even so, as simple as collecting early views may sound, there are a few bewilderments lying in wait to confuse collectors, especially if a card comes in what is termed a multi-category. Surely, it is frequently argued, lighthouses, windmills, watermills, post-offices, trams, railways, shop-fronts, piers, fire-stations, children bowling hoops, etc., etc., must come under the general heading of topography? Indeed they do, but they also come under more specialized subjects as well, and some of those subjects are scarcer to find than others, making them, of course, more expensive. Many a dealer has been faced with the poser of where to put what when confronted with a postcard with a post office in the foreground, a railway station which can just be glimpsed at the back, and a reasonable view of a tram travelling down the middle. So a choice has to be made between three different classifications.

Then there is the hairy problem of pricing view cards. Why, ask so many collectors, are common cards becoming so costly? This depends on how common is common. Common to the postcard dealer, would be a view he has seen so many times he begins to wonder whether any were sold in the first place. But generally speaking, scenes of churches, municipal buildings, museums, beaches, and most views of city centres are considered to be common, and none of these will be overpriced by reputable dealers who are usually only too pleased to be rid of them. A real

27

photographic postcard, however, which shows a good street scene in a place where Edwardian photographers did not descend in their droves is a prize well worth the extra premium charged. In fact, any photographic card which was not mass produced will be worth every penny.

How to start collecting view cards

Newcomers to the postcard-collecting scene are always puzzled about what to collect and how to go about starting. They have heard so much about how absorbing the hobby can be; the people next door collect what they call 'glamour' cards; colleagues at work are always going on about their railway or military collections; the milkman is a shipping fanatic, and there always seems to be a drinking acquaintance down at the local who has a bundle of postcards which he has just happened to acquire from a 'dear old lady' who thought they were worthless. All very perplexing, until the truth dawns that of all the hobbies in the world, collecting old picture postcards is the easiest to master without having to wade through a mountain of reference books in search of knowledge. And like its associate pursuit of philately postcard collecting gives the joy of freedom of choice to specialize in any theme or subject at the personal whims of the collector.

The soundest advice to beginners is to concentrate on collecting views relating to the areas in which they live and work. From this modest base there will soon emerge a very wide choice of themes to suit individual tastes, and it will not be long before the new collectors will be chatting away to other enthusiasts as though they had been collecting postcards since they were first invented. But where are these postcard treasures to be found? Almost everywhere – but to help novice collectors an index of *internationally* known dealers appears at the end of this book. However, it is not unusual nowadays for postcards to be found at local stamp shops or antique dealers, whilst the weekly magazine, *Exchange & Mart*, runs a special advertising column under the heading 'Picture Postcards', which gives a highly informative guide to the needs of both dealers and collectors alike.

So, having solved the problem of how to start collecting picture postcards and from where they can be obtained, we now come to the question regarding the cost of this new-found hobby. The short answer is, as little or as much as personal budgets will allow. If newcomers have been ill-advised to go for cards – especially some of the more important artist-signed ones which have already gone through the ceiling of recognized catalogue prices – collecting postcards will soon become a very expensive proposition. But for those who are prepared to allow their feet to guide them along the less-frequented pathways the rewards in both pleasure and profit can be very satisfying. Like all collecting pursuits, the real fun lies in the hunt and the tracking down of items which follow unusual and individual themes, and the satisfaction of finding elusive additions to personal collections is immense. But with well over 2,000 categories of subjects from which to choose, there can always be found a theme obscure enough not to have been spotted by too many other collectors.

In early view cards alone, the scope for fresh collecting themes has by no means been exhausted. Interiors of ships, hotels, and shops can still be acquired for a few pence from dealers who have not yet seen their potential; to these can be added the views of quiet back streets of towns and cities, early inns which flaunt legible signs, or old-fashioned bathing huts on deserted beaches. Many a dip into boxes filled with postcards of churches and castles can often reveal an interesting gem which has been overlooked by busy dealers, such as a fine view of a horse-drawn vehicle parked outside a church or castle gate, for example. A card like this very often deserves a place in the more expensive transport section, so would be well worth the give-away price marked on the back.

But for both novice and the more seasoned postcard collectors, the greatest interest in early topographical cards is due to the mammoth changes in topography itself. All over the world buildings have been torn down: whole streets demolished, and in places where once the cattle grazed and wild flowers grew in colourful profusion, new housing estates and shopping precincts have mushroomed almost overnight. Changes have been swift, and mostly unacceptable to those who have had to live with them over the past couple of decades, so it is not surprising that the nostalgia cult has aroused so much interest. Early postcards showing buildings and streets long since vanished have brought comfort to the people who can remember them, and incredulous looks from those who have been born and bred to believe that tower blocks and supermarkets have always been part of the normal scenery. But though the changes may be an ill wind to some and not especially important to others, they have certainly not escaped the notice of the astutely enterprising collectors who have used specialized collections of postcards to produce monographs on an ever-increasing number of towns and cities. In addition, many of the editors of local newspapers are only too pleased to reproduce early views of their own locations provided a positive theme is there to enthral their readers.

Real photographic view cards

The fascination for early views has not gone unnoticed by amateur photographers either, particularly those who also happen to be collectors of picture postcards. Many a sunny day has been spent seeking the exact spots where Edwardian photographs were taken and then snapping the scenes as they stand today. This taste for developing 'Then and Now' compositions is beginning to become a craze all on its own, but the marriage between two engrossing hobbies, photography and postcard collecting, illustrates perfectly how a combination of interests can become intertwined. And again, of course, there is the bonus for camera-happy postcard collectors who are prepared to persuade editors of magazines and newspapers to see the readership value of publishing photographic relics of the past when they appear side by side with the present-day tokens for posterity. Nor are newspapers the sole medium for this theme. The entire range of the Gibraltar definitive postage stamps from $\frac{1}{2}$p to £1 values show, side by side, the same views as they were in Victorian times and as they are today. But while the demand for action-packed photographic views is brisk, there is also a concentration of interest in Edwardian photographers whose work can be identified by name. F. G. O. Stuart, noted for his English scenes of Hampshire, Lloyd Albury for rare views of Surrey, Henry Taunt of Oxfordshire, and the enigmatic Frenchman who merely describes himself as L.L. are among the names which immediately come to mind whenever such photographic cards are mentioned.

L.L. was a bit of a 'Scarlet Pimpernel'. His globe-trotting activities took him and his camera to many places foreign to his native shores with no one quite knowing where or when he would turn up next. But such is the clarity and sparkling animation of his work, it is instantly recognizable even before those tell-tale initials have been sighted. And how those initials have tantalized the devotees of the work of L.L. So frustrated was one collector he dubbed them to mean 'Little and Large' and so ended the speculation as far as he was concerned.

Then in December 1974 the co-author of this book, Valerie Monahan, purchased at a Phillip's of Bond Street auction, an album for the world-record-breaking sum of £2,200. The 797 postcards in it were mainly of political significance and had originally belonged to a Miss Maude Simpson who was reputed to have been a member of the Suffragette movement. And one of the cards in this collection revealed at least part of the answer to the mystery of the initials L.L. Figure 5 shows a beautifully posed picture of the Russian Royal Family photographed in 1901 by L. Levitsky and published by the Neurdein Bros. of Paris. So it is now reasonably safe to assume that the initials L.L. as shown on the comparative illustration of 'The Baths' at Eastbourne represent the name L. Levy (in Russian Levitsky) and as the first initial most probably stands for Louis, the name Louis Levy scans very well.

Collecting the work of named photographers is another sound suggestion for a theme upon which newcomers to the hobby could base the start of their collections for most postcards in this category, including L.L.'s, are in plentiful supply and accordingly are moderately priced.

La Famille Impériale de Russie. — N.D Phot

PHOTOGRAPHIÉ À PETERHOF LE 16 AOUT 1901
PAR L. LEVITSKY
PHOTOGRAPHE DE LL. MAJESTÉS

NEURDEIN FRÈRES, ÉDITEURS
— PARIS —
REPRODUCTION INTERDITE

Figure 5

Figure 6

33 EASTBOURNE. — The Baths. — LL.

There is so much to learn from the early Edwardian photographic views. The depiction of the fashions, habits, transport, and the political climates of the times has provoked many a student of social history to write with eloquence on the subject. Even so, it is difficult to find postcards showing views of the less salubrious areas in which the majority of people lived. Professional photographers tended to concentrate on the more aesthetic aspects of what was fashionable and picturesque rather than record the grimy drear of the back streets. Yet, the pathos and the comedy of the less conventional mass of Edwardian life somehow managed to thrust its impudence upon unsuspecting cameramen just in time for the 'take', thus injecting a spot of instant realism into what otherwise would have been a too carefully posed picture. Discriminating publishers were quick to see the value of photographing life as it happened, and busy street scenes teeming with humanity and traffic soon became more popular than the contrived views of deserted beauty resorts which must have been taken either at first light or during the 'off season', since they rarely showed any sign of human interest or habitation. By 1903, when the craze for collecting picture postcards had become an international pastime for millions of people, postcard albums were beginning to resemble a positive kaleidoscope of the colour and action of the so-called gaiety of the Edwardian age.

And when it is remembered that collecting picture postcards in those days was a matter of unfeigned delight without thought, or even desire, to confine collections to any particular theme, it will be understood by present-day addicts for collecting postcards why early albums tended to be interspersed with a profusion of greetings for birthdays, Christmas, Easter, and the New Year, meandering through an extravagance of views and comic cards to the excitements of finding the scarcer gems of Art Nouveau and whatever may be currently in collectable vogue today. It must also be remembered that in those days, when collecting picture postcards first held the world in its thrall, that the ways of human caprice were also unchanged! No one in those days had a thought to spare for posterity; no one filled their postcard albums with earnest considerations about the possible increases in value which their postcards might mean to any future generation. Picture postcards, in those days, were pasteboard frivolities to be preserved in much the same way as instant colour photographs and home movies of memorable holidays and events are kept now. And just like today, crazes came and went – only the fun and fashion for collecting picture postcards has proved to be not quite as ephemeral as others.

Who among those early collectors could have forecast that pictures of railway stations, sights of ceremonies to commemorate the laying of the new tram-lines, the jovial smiles of straw-hatted purveyors of meat beaming beside great hunks of beef, mutton, and pork hanging outside many a local butcher's shop, could provoke the slightest stir of curiosity in those who were to be born in an age when the advanced technologies of man allowed him to glide across the surface of the moon? To those early Edwardian collectors, the idea that the postcards which had cost them only a few pence could ever be contemplated as future propositions for investment would have been quite ridiculous. And yet, that is exactly what the really early postcards have become. Real photographs of railway stations, on-the-spot pictures of accidents and disasters, close-ups of Edwardian shop-fronts displaying wares which are unheard of in today's supermarkets, scenes of lively street markets and thoroughfares, and close-ups of every kind of early transport vehicle – all of these and many others are among the most desirable pictures on postcards sought by the collectors of today, and most of them have high rarity factors in terms of price.

Artists' impressions of views in oil-paint and watercolour

Until about the middle of the Edwardian period when the 'Autochrome' method of photographic colour-printing was adopted for postcards, the processes used for colouring photographic cards were done by hand, either by tinting or using a colour-wash system. But by 1900 the many artist-signed postcards produced on the continent of Europe and the superb colour of the chromolithographic-printed cards produced in Germany were becoming increasingly attractive, and after the British had seen the first artist-signed battle scenes of the Boer War by Richard Caton-Woodville and Harry Payne there was a tremendous demand for coloured cards in Britain.

By the turn of the century, Messrs Raphael Tuck and Sons had already established with great success their famous 'Oilette' series. For some thirty-odd years before the beginning of the picture postcard craze, Raphael Tuck's had been publishers of fine greetings cards and Valentines and they had already earned the honour of being granted the Royal Warrant by Queen Victoria in recognition of the quality and excellence of their work, an honour which was later to be ratified by King Edward VII. But as well as being able to display the Royal crest, Tuck's had also devised an ingenious trademark which became an international symbol of incomparable craftsmanship and reliability. This same symbol of artist's easel and palette appeared on all the picture postcards produced by Tuck's, and, of course, since only the best artists were commissioned by them, their symbolic trademark was even more appropriate.

Tuck's 'Oilette' series were usually published in sets of six, each card and set inscribed with individual numbers so that accurate records could be kept by collectors who were given every encouragement by Raphael Tuck & Sons to collect Tuck postcards – for the quality and excellence of their products were well matched by the company's business acumen and expertise. It was Messrs Raphael Tuck & Sons who ran the very first postcard competition, offering £1,000 to the collector who could show the largest collection of Tuck's postcards which had been postally used. The announcement was made for this competition in the very first edition of *The Picture Postcard Magazine* to be issued by Mr E. W. Richardson, a British journalist who had foreseen the potential of picture postcards, and for 2d per monthly issue it was packed with well-informed articles and other items of interest to Edwardian collectors.

The famous 'Oilette' range of picture postcards covered a prodigious range of subjects, including thousands of topographical views of practically every country in the world, and all of these postcards were painted and mostly signed by the top scenic artists of the day. The names of artists commissioned by Raphael Tuck & Sons are too numerous to detail here, and as most of Tuck's records were destroyed during the Second World War it is doubtful whether even the most comprehensive list could ever be proved to be complete. But we certainly think that a good selection of some of the more notable names should be cited with the type of work they painted. Artists like:

Charles E. Flower – noted for his highly detailed views of London, York, and Winchester, and many other English cities.

G. H. Jenkins – who chose Devon and Cornwall for most of his settings.

Henry Wimbush – particularly enjoyed painting lakes, but also produced a prolific number of town and city views of Scotland and England.

A. Bridgeman – another artist to concentrate on Devon scenes.

G. E. Newton – who captured the drama of rough seas.

M. Morris – another artist who was fascinated by the stormy waters as shown in his series 'What are the Wild Waves Saying?'

A. L. Pressland – had a penchant for painting garden scenes.

Hadfield Cubley – painted Shropshire and Cheshire views.

Henry Stannard – was a very fine landscape painter.

W. Mathison – mainly views of London.

Jotter – who rarely signed his real name (Walter Hayward Young) was one of the most productive artists, who worked for many publishers including Raphael Tuck & Sons, and his work covered a large proportion of the British Isles.

Professor Van Hier – was a most accomplished artist of misty winter scenes, rural aspects, and sunsets.

F. W. Hayes – mainly preferred to do landscapes of North Wales.

Harry Payne – was most famous for his military sketches, but he also painted a number of very fine series of rural views – farming, horses, etc.

36

Arthur Payne – the brother of Harry (and they often joined forces when they were painting), preferred to draw and paint cathedrals and castles.

As well as the many 'Oilettes' of British scenes, Tuck's produced a number of specialized series of American towns and cities, European countries, the Commonwealth, Russia, China, and Japan. And as if this was not sufficient to bring the world to every doorstep, they went ahead with publishing the 'Wide, Wide World' series to illustrate not only topography, but also the diverse ethnologies of the numerous lands they described.

But although Raphael Tuck & Sons were the acknowledged leaders in the picture postcard publishing world, there were many other publishers who were very much aware of the commercial potential offered by employing artists to paint specialized work for them. J. Salmon of Sevenoaks in Kent produced an enormous number of postcard sketches in watercolour, some of the finest examples of which are by A. R. Quinton who worked exclusively for Salmon's from 1912 until he died in 1934. Quinton's work is now greatly appreciated by present day collectors, mainly for the clarity of detail and an immaculate use of colour – in fact, his sketches for picture postcards are so good they could almost be photographic. There were many other artists whose work was produced under the Salmon's banner; W. W. Quatremain is known for his excellent views of towns; C. Essenhigh-Corke for fine drawings of both exteriors and interiors of country houses, and a number of scenes of British counties; Harold Laws, Wilfred Ball, W. Dyer, and many more can be counted as artists of merit whose work is beginning to be eagerly sought today.

In this field of artists' impressions of how the world looked in the Edwardian age, the opportunities for new collectors to build respectable collections are endless, and apart from these cards being attractive enough in their own right, there is the supplementary charm of none of them being beyond the reach of those who do not possess bottomless purses! From the glorious sunsets produced by Hildesheimer to the bleak scenes of the Highlands painted by Alfred de Breanski and posthumously produced by C. W. Faulkner, the choice for even the most individual of tastes is the widest possible. In fact, the length and breadth of an Aladdin's cave of absorbing artistic wonders lurks waiting to be discovered in every shoebox of topographical postcards paraded by dealers at stamp and postcard fairs or in any shop where picture postcards are sold. The only requirement necessary is the patience to spend the time to wade through the classifications of counties and countries which could involve the scrutiny of many thousands of postcards, but the reward will probably be that more cards will be found than can be afforded at face value – in which case, here is a tip, set aside every card that appeals, then ask the dealer to give an over-all price for the lot. Usually when collectors are prepared to purchase in reasonably bulky lots considerable reductions in price can be expected and are usually given by reputable dealers.

Publishers of early view cards

Since the revival of the craze for collecting picture postcards in 1970, most of the interest has converged upon the multi-categories of the pictures themselves. But a new fashion for collecting particular publishers is beginning to emerge, and again this is a range which allows much freedom of choice for novice collectors who may have a fancy for specializing. There are, as can be imagined, a large number of manufacturers of picture postcards, many of whom were not quite as famous as others. Still, whatever the fame or obscurity of any of the Edwardian publishers, nothing can dim the undeniable quality of most of the postcards they produced. While most of the well-known publishers made it their business to ensure that their own productions of view cards reached the widest possible markets via the large and small stationers shops and the automatic vending machines which were to be found at most railway stations and the lobbies of the more important hotels, the smaller printers were just as satisfied with their share of a more localized trade. And it is in the area of collecting locally printed postcards where collectors can mostly be the winners, for not only are such cards cheaper than those published by the better-known publishers, they can also be considered to be limited editions since none of them ever came into the mass-produced range.

There were, of course, literally thousands of local publishers and printers producing postcards in whichever part of the world they happened to live and work. Most of them were sufficiently obliging to publish their names and place of origin or business on the reverse side of the cards, so for collectors who have discovered a liking for postcards published by the lesser-known printers, the process of finding them is simple. A random selection from our own topographical collections brings to light a few examples of the type of postcard to look for – R. Wilkinson & Co., Trowbridge, Wiltshire, photographed and published Wiltshire views; F. Jenkins, Post Card Publisher, Southwold, concentrated upon purely local cards of Southwold; Fred Spalding, Photographer, Chelmsford, spread his net around Essex; the 'Williams' Series, 152 Bell's Road, Gorleston-on-Sea, also went in for solely the local scene; W. Shaw, Burslem, published Staffordshire views, and E. Metcalfe, Post Office, Merstham, printed both sepia and tinted views of Surrey. Searching for localized publishers can be great fun and certainly adds zest to collecting topography – especially when it is discovered that some of these home-spun products are equal in quality to many of the postcards produced by the more illustrious manufacturers.

Although most of the early publishers of postcards did not confine their activities only to publishing view cards, we thought it would be less confusing to readers if the compilation of the following list was limited to the names of those publishers who are widely recognized in the topographical field – even though some of them will again be mentioned in the chapter on thematic subjects.

Blum & Degen (trademark 'B & D') of London – instituted in 1895, this firm produced distinctive vignette views on blue card, later allowing the picture to take up the whole of the space available after the standard size of postcard was introduced on 1 November 1899. In the early years they produced many thousands of cards, many of which are still to be found today.

Jesse Boot, Nottingham – started publishing postcards in 1901, using their trademark, 'Boots Cash Chemist'. Most of their early cards were in sepia or black and white, but later, under the new heading 'Boots "Pelham" series', they ventured into colour printing.

Delittle Fenwick & Co., York (D. F. & Co. or Defco) – entered the postcard market in 1903, and their 'views' were extraordinary 'moonlight' versions of British scenes which were quite obviously photographed in daylight, and later covered in a blue-wash with the addition of a 'moon' which never quite seemed to be in the right place; But nowadays, Defco 'moonlight' views are amusing to collect.

E. T. W. Dennis & Sons, Scarborough – another firm which started up in 1901, publishing many fine views as well as a number of colourful novelty postcards with concertina-pullouts of miniature views attached.

C. W. Faulkner & Co., London – long before the production of picture postcards, Messrs Faulkner & Co. were linked with the firm S. Hildesheimer producing Victorian greetings cards, etc., but in 1900 Faulkner's started producing picture postcards, although their output of views was not as prolific as the number of delightful themes they introduced.

F. Frith & Co., Reigate, Surrey – concentrated solely on view cards from 1902 onwards. Mainly sepia and tinted cards.

Gale & Polden Ltd, Aldershot, Hampshire – mostly publishers of very fine military and naval postcards, but they also published views.

F. Hartmann – not only started publishing postcards in 1902, but also introduced the more convenient type of postcard with the divided back on the address side of the card. Apart from full-view postcards, this firm also produced multi-view type cards.

S. Hildesheimer & Co., London and Manchester – published many colourful views of rural scenes, sunsets, etc., from 1902.

40

Ja-Ja – are mainly known for their beautiful full-out crests of towns and cities, and the clan tartan series, but a few views can also be found under this name.

Jarrolds Ltd, Norwich – were among the early starters in 1898, and many of their excellent quality views were painted by 'Jotter', Walter Hayward Young.

Judges Ltd, Hastings, Sussex – mainly moderately priced sepia views of the south of England.

Knight Bros came into being in 1904 with innumerable cards, including a great variety of views.

Millar & Lang (trademark National Series) – another firm noted mainly for high-quality cards of a thematic nature. Instituted in 1903, they produced a few examples of excellent view cards.

R. P. Phillimore & Co., Berwick – was one of the better-known private firms formed for the purpose of producing Phillimore's own very fine drawings of views.

Photochrom Co., London & Tunbridge Wells – established in 1902 – were responsible for the delightful 'Celesque' and 'Wedgwood' series of views.

Pictorial Stationery Co., London – was another of the early starters, first publishing postcards in 1896. Their range of very beautiful views in the 'Peacock' series are still to be found at most moderate prices.

Regal Art Publishing Co., London – was founded in 1903, adopting a format for their views very similar to the postcards issued by Raphael Tuck & Sons.

J. W. Ruddock & Sons, Lincoln – specialized in fine watercolour views of Lincolnshire from 1904.

J. Salmon, Ltd, Sevenoaks – was first established around 1880, but did not diversify into postcards until 1900. This firm is still one of the leading postcard publishing firms today and, with the excellence of the past work of artists like Quinton and Quartremain to show as examples, the work they presently produce takes a lot of beating.

George Stewart, Edinburgh – are the claimants to the distinction of publishing the very first British views of Edinburgh in 1894.

Stewart & Woolf, London – were producing some of the finest postcards ever seen by 1904, including a number of rural views.

A. & G. Taylor, London – produced a number of views of an indeterminate date. This firm also claimed to be 'By Appointment to her Late Majesty'.

Raphael Tuck & Sons – established in the early 1870s, holders of the Royal Warrant to Queen Victoria and later Edward VII, first produced postcards on 1 November 1899. Tuck's are notable for thousands of very fine series of view postcards which were produced both in colour and black and white. From July 1900 all their series were numbered, starting with twelve coloured views of London as Series 1. This firm also published a staggering number of international scenes.

Valentine & Sons, Dundee – can be traced back to the 1840s when they published pictorial envelopes, including the designs for the 'Ocean Penny Postage', but it was not until 1897 that they began to produce picture postcards. In addition to publishing countless photographic cards, they also held the official concession to produce postcards for all the major exhibitions held in Britain, such as the Franco-British, Japan-British, etc.

J. Welch & Sons, Portsmouth – were producers of tinted photographic views of Hampshire from 1903.

Wildt & Kray, London – concentrated principally on producing greetings cards, but they also published views from about 1906.

J. E. Wrench, London – one of the most enterprising firms to produce high-quality postcards in 1900, including the valuable 'Links of Empire' series.

British publishers, it seems, followed the theory that it paid to advertise, which is the main reason why it has been possible to list them. But the manufacturers of overseas views are not quite so easy to identify, most of the French views bearing nothing but the inscription 'Carte Postale', and the same shy anonymity applies to most other continental countries. Those who did manage to overcome their charming but nevertheless irritating predilection for self-effacement did so by conceding the barest details, usually printed in the smallest possible type, centrally positioned on the reverse side of their postcards. Austria, Germany, and Switzerland, however, proved to be the exceptions, for the publishers of their excellent products always displayed on one side or the other the names and addresses of those responsible for their production.

The United States of America also exercised an excess of discretion regarding the publishers of their view cards, but a browse through American topographical picture postcards will constantly divulge the names of the more prolific publishers. Names such as the Detroit Publishing Co., Curt Teich & Co., Chicago; The Souvenir Postcard Co., New York; E. C. Kropp, Milwaukee; Aero Distributing Co. Inc., Illinois; Hornick Hess & More, Sioux City, Iowa; I. & M. Ottenheimer, Baltimore; Metropolitan News Co., Boston; Edward H. Mitchell, San Francisco; A. C. Bosselman & Co., New York; V. O. Hammon, Chicago and Minneapolis; American News, New York; H. C. Leighton, Portland, Maine; and the Illustrated Postcard Co., New York. But since there are a number of view cards featuring every single State in America, there must be countless other publishers of American topography.

From this will be seen an almost infinite variety of collecting themes in the publishing field alone, and while some collectors will concentrate upon collecting the sole works of one publisher, others will be more intent upon gathering in single examples of all the different names of postcard manufacturers that they can discover – and just think of the collection this idea would form, as well as the absorbing hours to be spent comparing the different qualities and techniques of printing employed by the publishers of such a unique hoard.

Matching postmarks with the view

Apart from the obvious attractions of the pictures on the fronts of postcards and the photographers, artists, and publishers who were responsible for their production, there is an even more profound interest to be brought to the notice of novice collectors – and even some of those who are more advanced.

Postal historians who for so many years lodged querulous objections to the invention of picture postcards, now acknowledge them to be part of the postal system. At every postcard fair and place where postcards are sold there will be seen the dedicated collectors of postal history poring over bundles of postcards – usually with magnifying glasses at the ready! They are a wily lot compared with collectors who are only interested in the picture aspect of postcards, and they are adept at concealing their glee when they find valuable postmarks tucked among the cards which have been lowly priced by unsuspecting dealers. In fact, such is the artfulness of some of the seekers after postal history gems, they are not above scolding postcard dealers for over-pricing cards which they know only too well are often worth pounds more than the pence being charged.

But although the complex world of identifying the more desirable postal marks will be beyond the average range of people who are only just beginning to grasp the mechanics of collecting picture cards, there is an uncomplicated way for them to enjoy a simple mixture of both spheres. Hunting for postmarks which correspond with the place names of the views on the picture sides is a good start – and from this will evolve a more inquisitive interest in the differing shapes and sizes of the postmarks themselves. Squared circles, duplex marks, thimbles, single and double circle C.D.'s (city date stamps), skeletons, hammers, hooded circles, and a host of other odd postmark names will mean very little to the beginner. But as they progress, with the dual interest of collecting postmarks to match the view, so will the urge to learn more about postmarks become more persistent – especially when it is discovered that some of them are valuable.

This will be the time when a copy of *Picton's Priced Catalogue of Pictorial Postcards and Postmarks* will come in useful. Compiled by Mr Maurice R. Hewlett, this book not only illustrates many of the postmarks which the novice finds puzzling, but prices them as well. Naturally, the scarcest postal marks to find are also the most expensive to purchase, but it is still possible to be lucky enough to discover some of the treasures avidly sought by postal historians and philatelists. Old postcard albums acquired direct from either the original owners or their relatives will often disclose Railway T.P.O.'s (Travelling Post Office marks), S.C.'s and S.T.'s (Sorting Carriages and Tenders), Paquebots and other ship marks, and it is even possible still to find a valuable Clyde Steamer mark or the highly prized private cachet of 'La Marguerite' of the Llandudno to Liverpool steamer.

But the postmarks most likely to make hearts beat faster are those which were designed to delay the delivery of Christmas Mail until 25 December. These special 'Posted in advance for Christmas Day' marks were in limited use between 1902 and 1909, and their value can be anything between £50 to £400. Examples of these Christmas cross marks are illustrated in the full-page illustration (Figure 7) with some of the other types which we thought would be interesting to readers.

It will, of course, be understood that the study of postmarks and stamps is a very wide subject upon which many erudite books have been written, and it would be wrong for us to suggest that collectors of picture postcards can assume that their hobby is in the same league as the postal historians. But, having said that, it must be added that an intelligent interest in the postal side of picture postcards is as much the prerogative of picture card collectors as anyone else.

Messages on the reverse side of view cards

Open communications written to one person from another on the message side of postcards cannot be considered in any way private – although the more sensitive collectors have admitted to some embarrassment when the occasional 'chronicles of Edwardian courtship' have come their way. The passionate declarations of undying love and the revealing secrets about how Edwardian lovers spent their more intimate moments together rarely, if ever, appeared on the backs of view cards. But that is not to say that the messages sent with the views were dull; not all were restricted

45

Figure 7. Christmas cross and other interesting postmarks of the period.

to dissertations on the weather or 'wish you were here' themes. Many absorbing and instructive hours can be spent with albums filled with postally used cards which have been acquired from private sources – especially when the postcards have been inserted in chronological order. The first-hand information, usually written with leisured eloquence, about the places visited is more inspiring to read than many of today's travel brochures. And in addition to the travelogues, so much can be learned about the character and manners of the writers of the postcards which used to be sent with such marvellous regularity – even as many as three or more cards are frequently discovered bearing same-day postmarks.

The most exciting discoveries are made when albums which once belonged to famous people are found. And when it is remembered that the craze for collecting picture postcards was a pastime shared by Royalty down to the lowliest kitchen-maid, such finds are not as unlikely as they may sound. The major difference, of course, is that the more discerning tastes of the rich and famous would be reflected in the type and quality of the postcards they collected, and although whatever they wrote to each other is of great interest, the potentially high value of the postcards themselves is more important! For it is in these albums that the beautifully printed early German 'Grüss aus' cards will be found, each with their monochrome or delicately coloured multi-vignettes of scenes of towns, cities and the more remote villages of Austria and Germany. And there will also be a profusion of early Tuck's views, American and European scenes, commemorative cards, and postcards depicting aspects of the Boer War and the Boxer Rebellion, and no doubt a seemingly endless selection of Art Nouveau. Unfortunately, most of the more fabulous collections have been purchased by dealers who are usually obliged to break them up, since few can afford to keep these collections intact for their own enjoyment.

Novelty view cards

After the first fine flush of the beginning of the postcard craze when collectors were quite content with the vast selection of postcards already on offer, publishers began to wonder how long the euphoria for collecting would last. Competition between them was already fierce – though friendly enough – but they all shared the common resolve to keep their businesses buoyantly prosperous, and so it was not long before they were each devising fresh – and sometimes quite outrageous – ideas to tempt even bigger and better custom. The award for the most atrocious invention must go to whoever thought of producing aluminium view cards. Quite naturally, the postmen complained that not only could the sharp edges of these cards inflict cuts to their hands, but also they could cause damage to other mail with which they came into contact, and so the Post Office issued a directive to say that aluminium postcards would only be delivered when enclosed in suitable envelopes.

The United States introduced a gentler type of novelty card in real leather, many of which showed painted views, and a number of these and similar Canadian ones can be found which have been through the post. Ireland came up with their peat views and other Irish scenes – these are an interesting novelty though their dark brown hue is not especially attractive. Messrs Valentine's brought out 'Giant' postcards which despite their size of $7\frac{1}{2}$ in. $\times 5\frac{1}{2}$ in. could still be posted at the $\frac{1}{2}$d British rate. The Rotary Photo Co. competed by going from the sublimely large to the ridiculously small or producing bookmark cards and the tiny 'Midget' cards. Then there were the panoramic views which were double the length of the standard-size postcard; stereoscopic cards which gave a 'three-D' effect when viewed through portable or box stereoscopes.

German firms delighted collectors with their new 'Hold-to-Light' (H.T.L.) cards. These came in three different styles: *Cutouts*, the most common of which is a black-printed view on blue card, with yellow windows (and usually a moon) which, when the scene is held to the light, glows with a night effect. *Chameleon transparencies* – which look so ordinary at first sight that they can easily be passed over as nothing more than a black and white view – but a closer look will reveal the invitation, in many varied

ways, to hold the card up to the light when 'you shall see a charming sight' and, sure enough, the black and white view changes the scene to a pastel-coloured hue. But by far the most splendid of the H.T.L. cards are the '*Meteor' transparencies* which are already superbly coloured views, which when held to the light are breathtakingly transformed. Usually 'Meteors' produce the most realistic glow to a daytime scene, but very often they will also reveal hidden figures or objects which cannot be seen until held to light.

The French introduced many of the composite sets, most of which were of a more thematic nature, but there are a number of sets of twenty-four cards or more which when properly assembled show views of cathedrals and other beautiful buildings.

But, perhaps, of all the view cards which had something more to offer than straightforward paintings or photographs, the woven silks produced by the two Coventry firms of Messrs Thomas Stevens, and Messrs Grant, are the most spectacular. Woven silk pictures and portraits had been in fashion since the 1840s, but it was not until 1879 that Thomas Stevens introduced the first of his brilliantly coloured Stevengraphs, and the postcard versions of views and portraits of famous people did not appear until the early part of the new century. The postcards produced by both W. H. Grant & Co., and Thomas Stevens were,

Figure 8

and still are, immensely popular with collectors. Both firms manufactured a number of superb views which at first sight closely resemble photographs – the Grant's example of 'Lister Park, Bradford' is illustrated in Figure 8, and it will be seen that the picture is bordered by a printed scroll design, the method which was used to distinguish Grant's products from the embossed or ribbed borders of the works of Thomas Stevens. But, attractive as these postcards are, they are not so easy to find and are rather on the expensive side.

Building a collection of views

Having once decided upon the location which is to form the nucleus of any topographical collection, the golden rule is to stick firmly to that decision. Whether that nucleus is Baltimore, Berlin, Birmingham, Bordeaux, or whatever, refuse to be tempted to stray too far outside the radius of the place originally chosen. Experienced collectors know only too well the follies of random buying, especially when postcards of other towns, cities and villages always seem to be so much more appealing than those featuring their own areas.

When visiting postcard fairs, bourses, or the known dealers in postcards, make sure that sufficient time can be spared to browse through all the stock available where particular interests are likely to be found. If luck is out as far as the general views of street scenes, etc., are concerned, then have a look through the transport sections, categories marked 'shop-fronts', post-offices, even the classifications of accidents and disasters. Any of these and many more could turn up gems relevant to specialized collections. Try as far as possible to store postcards in chronological order – easy enough when postcards have been postally used, thus giving the dates when views or events were photographed, but if the pictures on mint cards are troublesome to date, their origins can often be traced through reference books or visits to local museums. This really is a nicety to be seriously observed for it is most off-putting to find early Edwardian cards jostling side by side with unrelated views of the George V – or even the George VI – period.

The condition of postcards is also a most important factor to remember – especially as very few can be picked up for the proverbial song nowadays. Unless a postcard is found which is known to be so rare that it is unlikely ever to be seen again – and therefore acceptable in any condition – it is foolhardy to buy cards with corners missing, scuffed edges, unsightly creases, or which are generally grubby. Shop around, for finer examples will usually turn up in time.

But while the production of topographical postcards provided the mainstay of the postcard industry, there was also an enormous demand for a great variety of themes, and publishers were quick to respond by producing picture postcards to satisfy every taste and the strangest whims. Whatever there was to be seen of the life and times of over three quarters of a century ago, all was recorded – in one way or another, on a picture postcard!

3 *Thematic Postcards*

From 1902, many thousands of different kinds of postcards were published every day, and sold by the billion. Postcard dispensers, vending machines, revolving display contraptions, specially designed trays and shelves, all were packed to bursting with a multitude of themes to tempt every conceivable public taste.

Satirical humour, saucy comics, flag-bedecked patriotic and cruelly lampooned politicians, ingeniously devised novelty cards, romantic songs and sentimental hymns, colourful poster publicity, buxom beauties and glamorously slender ladies. Animals, birds, battle scenes and military uniforms, big ships, little ships, actors, actresses, and play pictorials, royalty, pageants, exhibitions, coin cards, stamp cards, reproductions of old paintings and the original work of new artists, and greetings galore for all conventionally recognized occasions. All of these themes, and many more besides, were to be seen on picture postcards in the days when filling albums was almost a religion. It was difficult for early collectors to concentrate upon collecting particular themes. So many of the messages on postally used cards ended up with, 'here's another for your collection – hope you like it', and whether it was liked or not, in it would invariably go into the next available slot in the postcard album.

Photographic views of disasters and accidents shared the same pages as hilariously funny comics; scantily clad ladies flaunted a brazen eroticism beside carefully composed pictures of royalty;

portraits of Edwardian actors and actresses competed with cleverly drawn caricatures; and the sensuously curving lines and scrolls of Art Nouveau would be seen midst a jumble of greetings cards and sepia views. And as incongruous as this sort of arrangement may seem to present-day collectors, no such thoughts appeared to trouble the minds of the original owners. To them, their postcard albums represented a kind of tapestry of their lives, woven with memories which reflected the happy times and the more sombre occasions. And the postmarks on the reverse sides of their cards provided all the chronological order necessary to jerk back those memories.

Although the pursuit of collecting any specific theme may not have been especially important, there was a great interest in collecting individual sets of postcards, and strict attention was usually paid to arranging these in their proper order. Mostly these sets when found in early albums are in mint condition for many publishers were obliging enough to issue them in printed envelopes inscribed with the titles and series numbers of each individual set. But there were other publishers who preferred to distribute their 'set-pieces' in small multiple editions, and much like some of the premium promotions of today, the hunt for the last card to complete a set would be a trial of patience to find. Even so, it all added to the fun of collecting picture postcards.

While most categories of postcards described as thematic provide enough material to warrant a whole procession of definitive books to be written about them, we must confine our enthusiasm to brief reviews of some of the themes which were so popular in the hey-day of postcards.

Art reproduction postcards

It has been suggested that browsing through a collection of reproductions of the famous paintings of old masters is rather like wandering round a 'poor man's art gallery' – if ever there was such a thing! Just the same, when these postcards were first issued, they cost much more to buy than most other cards. Those published by the continental galleries, such as the Musées du Louvre, Luxembourg, Marseilles, and the Paris Salon were priced at 3d and 4d each – prices not quite within the range of the 'poor men' of the day.

Yet the strange anomaly of these cards is that although a high value was put upon them when they were first produced, they are now among the lowest priced cards to be collected today. This must be good news for newcomers to the hobby who are looking for a colourful and distinctive theme with which to fill their first album. Collections of Misch & Co.'s 'World Galleries' series, reproductions by Stengel & Co., Dresden, Ernest Nister, and C. W. Faulkner, present a most satisfying sight. The glowing colours – beautifully printed on stout board – of the reproductions of paintings by Raphael and Rembrandt, Murillo, Battoni, Giorgione, Turner, Landseer, and Reynolds, to mention a few, give many an hour of inexpensive pleasure, for none of the reproduction postcards manufactured by the above publishers are costly to purchase. The Medici Society also published an extensive range of art reproduction cards, as did F. A. Ackermann of Munich, S. Hildesheimer of Manchester and London, the Photochrom Co. of Tunbridge Wells, the British Museum, and the National Gallery. The most desirable reproduction postcards, however, were published by Messrs Raphael Tuck & Sons – superb early creations with undivided backs which nowadays cost pounds rather than pence to buy, exquisite sets of 'Famous Painters', 'Gallery Pictures', 'Landseer's Masterpieces', and the lovely series by J. Bartolozzi.

Albums filled with carefully arranged art reproduction postcards show such charm and beauty that they make an ideal first experiment in themes for new collectors.

Art Nouveau postcards

In an article published in the September 1975 edition of *Postcard Collectors' Gazette*, C. W. Hill said, 'Most collectors can recognize an Art Nouveau postcard when they see one, especially if it has been designed by an artist whose name is familiar as an exponent of the genre. But defining precisely what Art Nouveau itself is, and by what characteristics it may be identified, is not a task for the faint of heart.'

It must not be supposed by collectors of Art Nouveau postcards that the enchantments of the 'New Art' began with designs on pieces of pasteboard – or even with the name Mucha. One of the earliest influences of Art Nouveau was portrayed by the American painter James McNeil Whistler, when he designed the Peacock room which can be seen at the Freer Gallery of Art, Smithsonian Institute, Washington. This was in the 1860s, just about the time when an Englishman by the name of Arthur Lazenby Liberty had also become a devotee of Art Nouveau design. And in 1874, when he founded Liberty's of Regent Street, London, he supported and encouraged the creation of Art Nouveau design by dedicating the name 'Liberty' to its cause.

By the 1880s, Walter Crane, the English illustrator of children's books, had developed a distinct Art Nouveau style, and so had Aubrey Beardsley with his beautiful gold-blocked cover designs of many Victorian books. William Morris and Arthur Mackmurdo were also early English exponents of the Art Nouveau cult, translating the new art on to fabrics and wallpapers. But from Scotland, emerged a man who was to become one of the greatest advocates of Art Nouveau. Charles Rennie Mackintosh started his business career as an architect in Glasgow, but soon became better known for his distinctive designs of furniture and jewellery. Mackintosh introduced a delicacy of colour and an economy of line into his work which was breath-taking in its simplicity. He and his wife, with two of their friends, formed a group called 'The Four', which was acknowledged by the famous Viennese Secessionists in 1897.

In France, M. René Lalique was producing a glitter of gem-encrusted Art Nouveau jewellery – combs, necklaces, brooches, and pendants, which were guaranteed to send the women of French society into a frenzy for his work – and one of his greatest fans was Sarah Bernhardt. It was Bernhardt who was responsible for putting the name of the Czech-born artist Alfons Mucha on

55

the map by becoming his most distinguished model for many of the posters he designed.

It was not long before the name Alfons was changed to Alphonse, and Alphonse Mucha became the toast of Art Nouveau circles in France. By 1897, the works of Mucha and many of his contemporaries were published on picture postcards. Signed postcards by such artists as Eugéne Grasset, Henri Meunier, Brunelleschi, E. L. Lessieux, Arpad Basch, Henri Boutet, Paul Berthon, Carl Jozsa, Gaston Noury, Nini Hager, and Eva Daniell, were greatly cherished by the new patrons of the 'New Art' – the more discerning collectors of picture postcards.

All of these artists were masters of the aesthetic lines of Art Nouveau, from the voluptuous curves of beautiful women with long flowing hair to the spirals and scrolls which formed the flowers and trailing greenery of the background, and all had their own very individual styles.

By 1900, the Munich arts magazine *Jugend* was illustrating many of the Art Nouveau designs, including those drawn by new, up-and-coming young artists. The most outstanding of these was Raphael Kirchner, who was born in Vienna in 1876. Many of his early postcards, published by Marcus Munk of Vienna, are unsigned, and it was not until he arrived in France at the turn of the century that he became famous. Kirchner always used Nina, his ravishingly beautiful wife, as his model, and the many sets of picture postcards he designed were soon eagerly sought by collectors all over the world. Sets existed with exciting titles such as 'The Harem', 'Marionettes', 'Demi-Vierges', 'Les Cigarettes du Monde', and 'Enfants de la Mer'. And all of these enchanting postcards were well within the reach of all the early collectors – for none of them cost more than 2d each in those days, and some even less. In fact in one of the *early* catalogues to advertise postcards there are to be seen 'Kirchner Albums' offered containing 150 different postcards of the 'celebrated artist' Raphael Kirchner, for the extraordinarily low price of 12s 6d. The value of such an album today would be regarded as priceless.

But Art Nouveau postcards, beautiful and desirable as they are,

are very much in the specialist class of collecting. They are also difficult to find and consequently very expensive. But this does not mean that new collectors should be deterred from looking for them; there are still bargains to be found, and there are some fine examples of the work of Mucha and Kirchner illustrated in the colour section of this book.

Aviation postcards

One of the earliest postcards to show early flight is the triple 'Grüss aus' view shown in Figure 9 of the balloon flown by Salomon

Figure 9   D. Burke

Andrée, Knut Fraenkel, and Nils Strindberg from their base at Spitzbergen on 11 June 1897. Their dream was to reach the North Pole, and they managed to fly some 400 miles towards realizing that dream as the diaries and undeveloped film proved when their bodies were discovered 33 years later in Arctic Russia.

Balloons and dirigibles were the earliest models of successful flight, but there were still the men who longed for wings like the birds, to soar into the air, gliding and swooping with graceful aplomb, and to land all in one piece. Men like Otto Lilienthal from Germany, who built his first gliding machine in 1891 and fell to his death in 1896, and the young Scot, Percy Pilcher had similar ideas which also proved fatal.

The myth that only birds were meant to fly was finally confounded when Wilbur and Orville Wright built a heavier-than-air machine, flew it, and actually kept the thing in the air for all of fifty-seven seconds in 1903. Two years later, in 1905, the Wright brothers startled the world even more when they made the first recorded flight which lasted for twelve minutes. Like the good news-hounds postcard publishers were, their photographers were on the spot to record this astonishing feat, and a new category for postcard collectors was born under the name of Aviation.

Even so, early aviation cards before Blériot made his spectacular flight over the English Channel in 1909 are not so easy to find. Understandably, the regular publishers of postcards were more concerned with topping up the supplies of already commercially proven themes and views. Aviation, after all, was in its infancy, and far too new-fangled a theme to attract the 'vast majority' of customers who were only just being weaned to take an interest in the motor-machine – let alone a moving wonder in the sky which may or may not catch on.

So most of the pre-1909 aviation postcards to be published were due to the enterprise of independent photographers who pedalled their bicycles or hiked down to airfields, set up their tripods ready to bury their heads beneath the black canopies concealing their cameras to record the comings and goings of the pioneer aviators. These recordings were then published in limited quantity by local printers, most of whom were so unused to producing postcards that neither their names nor those of the photographers responsible would appear. Not unnaturally, pride of place in many of today's aviation collections goes to these authentic but anonymous postcards, bearing postmarks earlier than July 1909.

M. Louis Blériot changed the whole aspect of aviation when he landed at Dover from Calais at 5.30 a.m. on 25 July 1909. Postcards to commemorate his extraordinary achievement were on sale the very next day. From that moment on, flying became an activity to be taken seriously. Aviation meetings were arranged, early aviators became the popular heroes of the day, and postcards by the thousand were published and sold to an eager wide-eyed public. Many of these are illustrated in the book, *L'Aéronautique à la Belle Époque* by Georges Naudet which was published in 1976.

Early aviation postcards generate that certain derring-do glamour peculiar to those pioneer flying days; nothing excited imaginations so much as the sight of those first bi-planes and monoplanes did, even though most of them looked like home-made box kites tied up with string, and were moreover rather dangerous to fly!

With the institution of regular aviation meetings Aero-Philately was born. The aviation meetings of 1909 and 1910 in northeastern France and the 1911–14 events in America had special postmarks franked on the address side, all of which post-cards are now particularly valuable. Then to celebrate the corona-tion of George V, the first U.K. aerial post came into being. Special postcards with aviation designs were published, imprinted with the regular halfpenny stamp, and became known as the 'Lon-don to Windsor' coronation air-mails. In 1912, the *Daily Mail* newspaper sponsored air tours of Great Britain. Picture postcards featuring the name of the newspaper and signed photographs of pilots such as Hamel, Ewen, Salmet, etc., were sold at aerodromes then flown to the next point of arrival where they were posted. These flown cards received a rubber stamp inscription in violet or black ink over the message space. All of these aerial flown post-cards are valuable and eagerly sought by present-day aero-phila-telists and collectors of aviation picture postcards alike.

Although the genuinely early aviation cards are expensive to purchase now, there are some excellent reproductions to be found which were published by the British Science Museum, and avia-tion magazines such as *Flight* – none of these are too costly. Messrs Raphael Tuck & Sons also produced some very fine sets of early aviation art studies. Tuck's 'In the Air', and the 'Famous Aero-plane' series are less costly than the 'Famous Airships' and their 'Educational' series, but all of these cards are well worth searching for with vigour.

Children postcards

Judging by the number and variety of postcards featuring children and their pastimes, the Edwardians must have been inordinately fond of their offsprings! In most albums there would be found a fair mixture of postcards depicting nursery rhymes, elfin games among the toadstools, drawings of pantomime characters, party games, children standing and children sitting, nice children, naughty children, and sometimes downright odious children. Most of the picture postcards in this class were artist-drawn and signed, and as with most other categories of postcards, some are more ardently sought today than others. In America, the 'Kewpie' doll cards drawn by Rose O'Neill are immensely popular, so are the 'Sunbonnet Children' designed by another American artist, Bertha Corbett, and the Gassaway caricatures of children. And the book written by one of America's most knowledgeable post-card collectors, Mrs Sally Carver, *The American Postcard Guide to TUCK*, illustrates many fine examples of eminently desirable sets published by Raphael Tuck & Sons which are avidly collected on both sides of the Atlantic.

The 'cut-out' series of 'Dressing Dolls' features not only the dolls, but gives two changes of clothing as well. The idea was for children to while away an hour or two cutting out the dolls, and then dressing them in the variety of clothes provided. Postcards of this and similar series are obviously scarce to find in mint and untouched condition. Sally also draws our attention to an especially rare series of 'press-out' designs produced by Tuck's; the complete set of 'Swinging Dolls' – how about that for a title produced at the turn of the twentieth century? – produces a mechanical effect of the doll actually swinging when properly assembled. Then there were the 'Toy Rockers', 'Merry Little Men', and 'A Model Cottage', series as well as those which have an unmistakable Art Nouveau tinged embellishment about them – the Tuck set No. 691, modestly named 'Art Satin' is quite definitely in the 'New Art' class.

And so are a number of other picture postcards in the category of the 'Children' range. S. Barham designed several postcards of children cavorting with lanterns or kneeling beneath an array of out-sized flowers, and, of course, the Barham versions of 'Peter Pan' and 'Where the Rainbow ends' are quite famous. Henrietta Willebeek Le Mair, the Dutch illustrator of so many beautiful children's books, also delights the discerning collectors of today. Her set of 'Schumann's Masterpieces' published by Augener, of Conduit Street, London, in 1912, is pure Art Nouveau, and well worth the ridiculously low sum of three or four dollars currently being asked. Other widely collected artists of children's themes are Ethel Parkinson, Agnes Richardson, Millicent Sowerby, Florence Hardy, Flora White, G. G. Wiederseim, Pauli Ebner, A. Nash, H. Marsh-Lambert, E. P. Kinsella, Susan Pearse, Mabel Lucie Attwell, and Margaret W. Tarrant. All of the postcards produced by these artists are in the highly desirable range, and most of them are well within a price bracket to suit the most modest of budgets.

By now, it may be wondered why the name Kate Greenaway has not been included among the famous artists of children's cards – particularly as Greenaway is perhaps the most famous name of all. The answer, quite simply, is that although there has been a fashion of some long-standing to reproduce on postcards many of the delightful Kate Greenaway designs which were published by Marcus Ward, Kate Greenaway, who died in 1901, was never commissioned to draw specific work for postcards. Nor was Henri Toulouse Lautrec and Aubrey Beardsley – but their work, like Kate Greenaway's, was also reproduced on postcards – work which was originally commissioned for other media, so – as shocking as it may sound – the reproductions of the designs on postcards of the early Kate Greenaway *folded* greetings cards, as appealing as they are, are not worth the large sums quoted in many of the current postcard catalogues. Aubrey Beardsley died young at the age of twenty-six in 1898, and the brilliant poster painter Toulouse Lautrec lived only for thirty-seven years until he also died in 1901. Neither of these artists did original work expressly designed for the postcard medium – and as exciting as their work undoubtedly is, it is difficult to imagine that reproductions of it on postcards can command the three figures in pounds presently being estimated. As well as the artist-drawn postcards, there were innumerable photographic studies of children produced, many of which show prissy and quite unnatural poses. But whether postcards are artist-drawn or photographic, the realm of children's subjects has much to offer both beginners and the more seasoned collectors who may be looking for new themes.

Comic postcards

Of all picture postcard categories, the comic card is the most widely collected. Ranging from satire, sly enough in its humour to raise a smile from the most cynically inclined, to the rich belly laughs evoked by the robust sauciness of the traditional comic card. The odd thing is, that the humour of yesterday is as crisply apt today as ever it was. The hilariously funny situations depicted by Tom Browne on the many series of postcards which were published by Davidson Bros are as up-to-date now as they were when they were first produced. The striped bathing costumes bursting with out-sized bosoms and bottoms drawn by Donald McGill are still good for a laugh; so are the McGill versions of drunks, acid-faced women, and curvaceous flappers. McGill was the master of the saucy postcard, but he was never offensively obscene.

Raphael Tuck & Sons and Davidson Bros were two of the early publishers who, judging from the list of first-class artists they managed to commission, had the pick of the members of the London Sketch Club at their disposal. And nowadays, postcards signed by such artists as Phil May, Dudley Hardy, Lance Thackeray, Percy V. Bradshaw, Will Owen, Harry Rountree, Ludovici, George Belcher, Lawson Wood, and, of course, Tom Browne, are all priced at a premium. The most desirable of these artist-signed postcards are in the 'Write Away' series, which have the beginning of a message imprinted alongside the illustration; the idea was for the sender to complete the message in his own words. One of the wittiest we have seen shows a convict sitting in his cell, with the message, 'I'm likely to be confined to the house for some time ...' which is followed by ... 'so can't meet you yet for that odd gin and lime!'

Not all the imprinted messages were followed with phrases which made sense, for example the message, 'I should be only too pleased to join you ...' goes on to describe in great detail the nature of a particularly unpleasant ailment endured by a chap living next door!

Millar & Lang, Stewart & Woolf, Wrench, Valentine & Sons, Hildesheimer, Inter-Art, Joseph Asher, and C. W. Faulkner also manufactured some very fine comic postcards, most of them by signed artists, and as there are well over one hundred such artists whose names appear on comic cards, there is scope for everyone in the artist-signed collecting field. The cost of such cards will range from pence to pounds but there are thousands of excellent comics to be found for a few pence in the unsigned sections of humorous postcards. And in this section there are several other themes to consider. An album filled with brightly coloured comic cards similar to those drawn by 'Crackerjack' makes a very cheerful spread to browse through on a cold winter's evening. Then there are sporting themes, motoring jokes, funny hats and hobbled skirts, jovial policemen, endless accounts of holiday humour, and drinking topics galore – just to mention a few of the subjects which collectors find fun to collect.

Disasters and accidents on postcards

From comedy we move to tragedy, and if the transition seems a little abrupt, all we can say is that apart from trying to arrange our brief thematic accounts in alphabetical order, we are merely emulating one of the more relentless patterns of life. Railway accidents, motor smashes, mining disasters, plane crashes, earthquakes, explosions, fires and floods, and ships foundering and sinking, are all part of the unexpected cavalcade of miseries lurking round the corner to turn laughter into sorrow. The Edwardian age had its fair share of horrifying incidents, and somehow or other there was always someone with a camera to take on-the-spot action pictures which would appear on postcards the very next day! With the exceptions of the San Francisco fire, the floods of Paris, erupting volcanoes, and the major disaster of the sinking of the R.M.S. *Titanic* in 1912, which were all recorded on postcards by the larger publishing firms, most of the disasters and accidents were photographed and printed on a local basis. From the postcard point of view, this puts many of these cards in the limited edition class – thus making them scarce to find and accordingly expensive to purchase. There are, however, very few collectors who concentrate solely upon collecting calamitous situations, but postcards of localized accidents and catastrophes add a certain grim interest to topographical collections.

Exhibition postcards

The earliest examples of Exhibition postcards collectors may occasionally find today will be those featuring the Eiffel Tower at the Paris Exhibition in 1889.

Much more difficult to find are the cards which were issued by the British Post Office in 1891 for the Royal Naval Exhibition. The focal point of this Exhibition was the specially built model of Eddystone Lighthouse. Delighted visitors were able to climb to the summit of the model where arrangements were made for them to purchase and post the first British pictorial postcards showing a vignette of the real Eddystone Lighthouse.

Views of the Columbian Exhibition in Chicago were the next to appear on postcards in 1893. Then in 1896, there were exhibitions recorded on postcards in Berlin, Geneva, and Nürnberg; in 1897 it was the turn of Brussels, Hamburg, and Leipzig, and, in 1898, Turin. The following year there were none of outstanding importance, but from 1900 when the next Paris Exhibition took place there was a constant flow of Exhibition postcards published annually from one place or another, right up to 1914. From the picture postcard side, only the early exhibitions are costly to acquire, but from a philatelic viewpoint, Exhibition postmarks are well worth collecting. And more for the edification of new collectors – although some of the more established ones may also be interested – we have listed the places and dates of the major exhibitions which took place between 1900 and 1914.

1900 – Paris; 1901 – Glasgow and the Pan-American; 1902 – Cork and Wolverhampton; 1903 – Earls Court; 1904 – Bradford, Earls Court, Nantes, and St Louis; 1905 – Earls Court and Liège; 1906 – I.R. Austrian, Marseilles, and Milan; 1907 – the Irish International and Liège; 1908 – the Franco-British; 1909 – Imperial International; 1910 – Brussels and the Japanese-British; 1911 – the Coronation Exhibition, the Festival of Empire at Crystal Palace, and Turin; 1912 – Düsseldorf and the Latin-British; 1913 – Ghent and Leipzig; 1914 – the Anglo-American.

The most prolific number of Exhibition postcards published were those produced by Messrs Valentine & Sons for the Franco-British and the Japanese-British Exhibitions, and provided these cards have not been franked with Exhibition postmarks, new collectors should have no difficulty in picking them up for a few pence each.

Fantasy postcards

This category is perhaps the strangest of all picture postcard themes. Cards showing innumerable babies being plucked from trees, fished out of ponds, gathered into baskets like so many apples, growing in the hearts of cabbages, flying in balloons, or crouched on miniature 'potties', are the most common type of fantasy postcard to find.

Vastly more difficult to track down are the extraordinary black and white Fantasy Heads. Ingeniously composed designs of nude girls erotically forming the faces of Royalty and Heads of State; macabre compositions of quite ordinary situations resembling skulls such as the card entitled, 'Lamour de Pierrot', where the faces of Pierrot and his pretty companion represent the eye sockets, their hands – centrally clasped – the nose, and a feather fan and the glasses of wine so cleverly arranged to appear as the hideously grinning teeth of the skull. The morbid notion behind

65

these skull postcards is intended to show the nearness of death – and since all the characters used in the ordinary situations are usually young and beautiful, and very often quite clearly in love, there must be a 'Romeo and Juliet' theme hidden somewhere too!

But while the nude girls sprawl and pose with amatory abandon over the faces of Edward VII, Abdul Hamid, Alphonse III, Leopold II, the Kaiser, and Napoleon, the face of Count Zeppelin is made up of balloons with two zeppelins to decorate his cap – perhaps he was not quite so noted for his love of the gentler sex! Not all fantasy cards follow way-out themes. Many of the Alphabet cards come under this heading. Famous Edwardian actresses can be seen posing against or draped around the letters of the alphabet, and sets of these are now greatly prized. Several of the early publishers adopted this alphabetical theme, so there are in existence a large number of sets of twenty-six cards in different series to locate.

Glamour postcards

Although it was not until after the beginning of the First World War that the term 'pin-up' was coined, Edwardian collectors were well served with regular supplies of drawings of elegantly dressed, seductively curved pretty girls. Some of these postcards have frequently been confused with Art Nouveau themes, especially the ones which tend to resemble fashion-plates. But the black-stocking-clad beauties of Leo Fontan, and the tantalizing drawings by artists such as Penot, Maurice Pépin, Jack Abeille, G. Mouton, Maurice Millière, Xavier Sager, and Suzanne Meunier, are in a class of their own. All of these can be described as truly glamorous portrayals of delectable women.

The American artist Charles Dana Gibson created the 'Gibson' girl. The first alluring poses for the 'Gibson' girl sketches were modelled by his wife, one of the beautiful Langhorne sisters. But it was the British actress Camille Clifford who put life into Gibson's 'girl' by creating a particularly slinky walk and adopting the Gibson-girl style in her musical shows. But of all the postcards depicting this girl, the Gibson heads produced by James Henderson are by far the most popular.

After the ethereal slenderness of the Gibson and the Kirchner girls came the more sensual beauty of the girls created by Angelo Asti. Reproductions of these voluptuous and extremely colourful beauties were published from the Asti originals by Raphael Tuck & Sons, and these postcards are very popular today, and not over-expensive to purchase.

There are, of course, countless other artists who concentrated upon the 'glamour' scene. The American publishers Reinthal & Newman produced many delightful drawings by such artists as Harrison Fisher, Philip Boileau, Charles Scribner, and Hal Hurst. And one of the joys of collecting postcards of pretty girls is that the price range is not now as frightening as it used to be. Postcards in this category now start from around 50p, reaching a ceiling of about £6 for cards by the top rank artists.

Greetings postcards

Just like today, greetings cards appeared in all shapes and sizes and in the widest possible variety. The early German cards are considered to be the most desirable. These were usually embossed and very often heavily gilded, and, of course, there were cards to celebrate every occasion. But one of the most popular themes today are the New Year cards showing little gnomes showering gold coins around as if they grew on trees!

Apart from the modern trend of producing folded greetings cards, the illustrations and subject matter have changed very little. The only real difference between today's folded offerings and the greetings postcards of yesterday is that postcards are collectable since they can be stored away in albums, while the folded types usually end up in a waste-paper basket after they have served their purpose! This is a pity, for many of the designs on modern greetings cards are so good they ought to be preserved.

Heraldic postcards

Small crests of towns and cities are often to be seen on topographical views. But a real collection of Heraldic postcards is something quite different. Raphael Tuck & Sons published a number of series of early Heraldic postcards, all of which are coveted by today's collectors. Beautifully coloured, gilded, and embossed side crests of English towns and cities with small sepia views at the top; superb sets of ten cards depicting the crests and scenes of Boston, Washington, and Philadelphia; and a splendid series of twenty-four brilliantly coloured crests and flags of different countries. Then there are the crested postcards produced by Ja-Ja. All of these display large centrally placed crests on vertical cards with gilded borders which combines the name Ja-Ja in the bottom left-hand corner. Apart from the many towns and cities represented in this series, the crests of England, Wales, Ireland, and Scotland can also be found. And in addition, Ja-Ja published a special series for the Scots entitled 'Clan Tartan', with the crests of each clan centrally placed against the appropriate tartan background.

Postcards of Heraldic interest make an excellent show, and are well worth considering by new collectors – particularly the Ja-Ja series of cards which are still to be found at reasonable prices – as an attractive adjunct to topographical collections.

Military postcards

From the beginning of the Boer War in 1899, subjects of military interest appeared on picture postcards, and apart from the obvious scope for portraying battle scenes and uniforms, the postcard was seen as an expedient means of distributing propaganda. While British publishers concerned themselves with manufacturing postcards designed to boost the morale of British troops, continental postcard producers backed the cause of Kruger, the Transvaal President, by flooding the market with anti-British cartoons. All of these cards are among the scarcer collectors' items and not very easy to find nowadays. Nor are the fierce cartoons depicting the Boxer Rebellion when groups of Chinese nationalists attacked the foreign embassies in Peking in 1900 and murdered

European missionaries and Chinese converts by the thousand. But the most horrifying war cartoons to be produced were those ·issued during the Russo-Japanese War between 1904 and 1905, a perfect example (Figure 10) shows a Russian soldier being gobbled up with relish by his Japanese enemy.

Figure 10

Battle scenes, sieges, and war propaganda cartoons, however, form only a small part of the military category of picture post-cards. The main interest of military themes lies in the artist-drawn displays of uniforms, badges, medals, and military action pictures. Raphael Tuck & Sons published a prodigious number of military series, many of which consisted of several different sets under the same title. There are, for example, twenty-four postcards in 'The Military in London' series which are divided into four separate sets of six postcards each. Harry Payne and Richard Caton-Wood-ville were the principal artists commissioned by Tuck's to design military postcards, and sets like 'How he won the Victoria Cross', 'Regimental Badges and their Wearers', the 'Red Cross', and the multitude of sets showing the uniforms of British regiments are exciting postcards to collect. Tuck's, of course, did not confine their military cards to the British scene, the American and Euro-pean forces were also prominently featured.

Another British publisher, Gale & Polden of Aldershot, produced one of the finest and the longest sets of military postcards. An advertisement to publicize the set of 'History and Traditions' is headed by, 'The British Army – POSTCARDS of every REGIMENT. Uniforms correctly reproduced in colours – with crest, history and traditions. The only Army postcards authorized by the War Office. Price 1d each, the complete set of 120 cards 7/6d.' To purchase the complete set of these cards today would cost something in excess of £150!

There are tremendous opportunities for new collectors to build up worthwhile collections of military postcards, not all of which need to be in the artist-signed or cartoon class to make them interesting. Real photographs of camp life and humour, family type pictures of soldiers in uniform, and, of course, clear strikes of camp postmarks, play a vital part in building up respectable collections. Assembling a collection of military postcards embodies a magic of its own, for in what other category can be found such a miscellany of emotion? Comedy, tragedy, romance, heroism, pomp, pageantry, discipline, and the frailties of humanity, all are there to encourage or console, to puff even more the outsized ego, or to bolster the timid, to conjure smiles or invoke sorrow, to acknowledge a pride of being loyal members of whatever the race, colour, or creed of whatever nation a military postcard represents – what more can be asked or expected of one single category.

Novelty postcards

The postcards in the novelty section are not so much browsed through as played with! There are so many cards with wheels to rotate, levers to pull, blinds to roll up or down, models to cut out and stand up, that the novelty classification could very well be redubbed the 'Toyshop' of postcards.

Decorating postcards with real hair, real feathers, sprinkling them with glitter or encrusting them with coloured bits of glass to resemble jewels, embellishing them with silks and satins or pieces of gingham, was an Edwardian innovation introduced by publishers who had already learned the commercial value of gimmickry. And it was not only the regular postcard manufacturers who jostled for recognition of their novelty wares. A fascinating series of 'Fab Patchwork' cards appeared produced by W. N. Sharpe of Bradford. The idea was that the silk patches on the picture sides should be removed and sewn to make patchwork cushion covers. Perfumed sachet cards with crinkly tissue-paper fronts painted with the flower of whatever fragrance the sealed sachet concealed enjoyed a limited popularity. The Callender Paper Mills in Ireland made a number of real peat cards. Then there were the adroitly produced folded Christmas postcards which, when opened, a yard or two of paper chain stretched out in merry greeting.

Max Ettlinger who started to publish postcards in 1901 was one of the most ingenious manufacturers of novelty cards. The most spectacular of his creations were the cards which showed droll heads with cigars stuck in their mouths. These cigars could actually be lit and would smoulder away in a most realistic puffing manner. Ettlinger's also introduced the squeaking cards to an un-suspecting world, pictures of animals, birds and children conceal a padded squeaking device which when pressed let out a sound which was guaranteed to amuse the children and annoy the adults.

Using unusual materials was also a fashionable trend followed by Edwardian publishers. Celluloid cards were popular for a brief period, but because of the brittle nature of the material, corners were easily cracked or chipped, and it is now rare to find speci-mens in pristine condition. Postcards made of real leather were an American innovation and were produced by the millions, but although they can be purchased in the United States for a few cents, they are fairly expensive to buy in Britain and the continent. Aluminium cards were – and still are – the most hideous of post-cards, but for collectors of novelty cards, it is necessary to have at least one example of an aluminium monstrosity in their albums. Wooden postcards are also mainly of American origin, but the Japanese perfected the ideas for wood cards by producing delicate marquetry designs using several different types of coloured wood. Raphael Tuck & Sons produced brilliantly coloured sets of postcards with a coarse linen finish in their 'Real Japanese' series – gorgeous scenes of Geisha girls.

Jig-saw puzzle cards were also firm favourites with the public, the most exciting of which were issued in boxes of six cards by Raphael Tuck & Sons. Figure 11 shows the reverse side of one such card, Tuck's 'Picture Puzzle Postcards' being intended for 'progressive puzzle parties, etc.'. The difficulty nowadays, of course, is to find cards with all the jig-saw pieces intact.

Figure 11

Gramophone record cards were produced by German publishers and also by Tuck's. The extraordinary thing about these cards is that although they can actually be played at the old '78' speed, the material used for the discs closely resembles the modern substances used today!

But of all the novelty inventions, perhaps the Hold-to-Light (H.T.L.) cards take pride of place in most collections of this genre. Transparencies with their colour – and even subject – changes capture the greatest admiration; ordinary monographic views are transformed into delicate pastel-coloured scenes; angelic faces or the jolly form of Santa Claus appear from behind Christmas trees; Cinderella, alone and forlorn in her kitchen miraculously changes into a beautifully dressed princess; ogres appear from nowhere to destroy a pastoral peace – all of these and many more are the enchantments in store when transparencies are held to the light. Then there are the puzzle type of H.T.L.'s introduced at the beginning of the First World War, 'Find the submarine' being one of the most classic requests, and sure enough, when held to light, a picture of ships sailing the calmest of waters will reveal the enemy submarine lurking somewhere below when the card is exposed to the light. Pretty snow-clad Christmas scenes of cottages and watermills nestling beneath the shadows of village churches with cut-out windows, moons, and even 'Merry Christmas' messages, will show an evening glory of lamplight when held to the more searching glare of the electric lamp. And for the newcomer to postcard collecting who may be muttering that acquiring such cards will most probably be beyond his pocket, we have good news, for only the transparencies are expensive to purchase, and even then, only when dealers have recognized them for what they are, for not all are as easy to identify as may be imagined.

Novelty postcards were produced to suit all tastes and pockets; comic absurdities with patches of sandpaper stuck to the more prominent places of the human anatomy invited recipients, 'to strike a match upon my patch'; Horniman's, the tea people, introduced the 'Frictograph' card which promised a 'startling result' when the card was rubbed with the edge of a 'silver coin' – and sure enough, a picture would appear; phosphorous cards glowed in the dark after the instructions of 'hold to heat and a picture will appear' were followed. Expensive mechanical delights were produced, some with a complex number of rotating wheels intended to impart all manner of information when properly used; kaleidoscopic cards followed the same principle; levers were pulled to reveal rude protrusions of tongues, smiles, grimaces, or roving eyes; Venetian-type blind effects were used to show the arts of dressing and undressing the female form; and literally in their millions were produced the common varieties of concertina pull-outs. Most of these would show a selection of up to twelve different sepia views folded into position behind an appealing coloured picture, but the most desirable are the Christmas types which boast festive scenes to conceal concertinas of colourful party games, Christmas menus, or short compendiums of carols.

Without any doubt, a collection of novelty postcards is guaranteed to capture immediate interest – and often are the times when novelty-filled albums have been used as secret weapons to warm up parties which have shown the initial signs of becoming potential flops – for who but the most unimaginative could resist the magic of a H.T.L. card, the intrigue of rotating wheels and pulling levers, or waggling two forefingers through a couple of holes placed where the legs of a pictured bathing beauty should be? And who could fail to be baffled by the cards which bear the instruction, 'Bring slowly towards the eye and watch effect'? – the effect usually being to see a couple posed with a respectable distance between them, ending up in a passionate clinch when the card is drawn slowly to the eye.

Certainly there are a thousand and one pleasures in store for the new collector who opts for collecting novelty cards as a chosen theme.

Patriotic postcards

This theme shows practically every land full of 'hope and glory'. As can be imagined the colour and variety of flags and coats-of-arms feature prominently on most patriotic postcards. But the full spate of such cards did not appear for Britain and her continental Allies until the First World War when Allied flags, bulldogs, and a flood of 'entente cordiale' hit the postcard scene. Before this war, patriotic postcards were inclined to be distributed solely within the confines of individual lands, and all of the postcard-producing nations had some cause or other which warranted the hoisting of their own particular 'flags'. The United States, however, had many occasions which were to be – and still are – commemorated annually. Many of these celebrations were recorded in sets by Raphael Tuck & Sons and are illustrated and described in the book *The American Postcard Guide to Tuck* by Mrs Sally S. Carver. There are at least five different sets of twelve cards commemorating

'Decoration Day', and others for 'Washington's Birthday', 'George Washington', 'Lincoln's Birthday', and several sets for 'Independence Day'.

Patriotism may be an old-fashioned word now, but in the days when nations unfurled their flags and flew them at full mast, the ugly humour of politics had not then intruded sufficiently to dim the loyalty and devotion the people felt for their lands. And it is interesting to observe how quickly the colourful postcard reminders of patriotism are passed over by present-day collectors, 'No one wants them', say the dealers, and, 'just not my scene', explain collectors. What a long way it still is to Tipperary, lumbered with old kit-bags full of troubles in search of clouds with non-existent silver linings.

Political postcards

The former British Prime Minister, Sir Harold Wilson, once said that 'a week in politics is a long time'. Researchers through batches of early political postcards could add the rejoinder, 'but times don't change much!' As postcards show, history has a habit of repeating itself over and over again. The arguments put forward by Joseph Chamberlain in the early part of the twentieth century about modifying the laws of free trade to give supreme preference to British colonies, provoked just as much bitter opposition as the controversy over Britain's entry into the European Community, the cries about prices rising and shortages being created were just as loud. Both Joseph Chamberlain and his son Austen had an aptitude for creating situations which made them immortal on postcards. Austen's tariff reform policy prompted Millar & Lang to produce several cartoons under the heading, 'When Father says "Turn", we all turn', showing whole families crammed into one small bed. Another set of cards ridicules Joseph Chamberlain's love of orchids by drawing his face amid a variety of the species.

Sir Leslie Ward, the famous caricaturist who used the pseudonym 'Spy', drew twenty-four political caricatures for the magazine Vanity Fair which were later reproduced on postcards.

75

A. Ludovici was another master cartoonist of the political scene, Lord Rosebery and Joe Chamberlain being the main targets for his satire.

French publishers were also fond of poking fun at their politicians on postcards. They had a penchant for celebrating the removal of their leaders by ignominiously depicting their departures by perching them on top of an odd conglomeration of their belongings to be hauled away by donkeys, elderly horses, or even ravenous-looking wolves. The whole effect, signified by today's standards, portrayed a successful day in the lives of 'Steptoe & Son' or similar merchants of rubbish. Some of the French artists of political cartoons to look out for are F. Chamouin, Nadal, Egor, and Fercham.

Like other categories, collectors of political postcards do not have to rely upon artist-drawn or signed cards to enhance their collections. There are a great number of real photographic cards of individual portraits of politicians and statesmen, as well as group photographs of cabinets and governments of the day. Nor do new collectors need to concern themselves overmuch about the cost of political postcards, for most of them come well within the range of fair and reasonable prices, although it must be expected that action shots of the Sydney Street siege in which Mr Winston Churchill was involved in 1912, and on-the-spot photographs of strikes and marches and other industrial unrest, will command higher prices.

The very desirable Suffragette postcards will also be a trifle on the costly side – especially if they are real photographs of Mrs Emily Pankhurst, either of her two daughters, or any other prominent member of the movement she founded. And even the Suffragette cartoons similar to the particularly nasty one illustrated in Figure 12, showing the prevention of hunger strikes by R. F. Ruttley are becoming increasingly expensive. But there is another point about suffragettes to be mentioned in respect of postcards. These very determined women who tied themselves to lamp-posts and railings, and prepared themselves to suffer the agonies and humiliations of prison to further their cause, made frequent use of postcards as the most convenient means of communication at their disposal. Obviously, their messages would not be as blatant as to say, 'Tonight, we are planning to blow up the House of Commons, so wear your best asbestos suit!' The

Figure 12

subtlety would read something like this, 'Hope you are well. Looking forward to meeting you outside the Abbey at 6 p.m. Don't be late, we are going to a party and Chrissy will be there.' Not all such messages are seen on actual Suffragette cards but mostly on quite ordinary nondescript types, so it is well worth trying to spot what may well turn out to be communications from one Suffragette to another on cards postmarked from 1906 when women became militant until the start of the First World War in August 1914.

Railway postcards

Collecting railway postcards is the ideal theme for those who used to haunt the stations to sniff the pungent scent of the steam with notebooks and pencils poised to jot down numbers and names and whatever else they found of interest. In the days when railway companies were privately owned there was tremendous scope for all kinds of pleasures in the train-spotting field. And those same companies were quick to take advantage of the advertising potential offered by postcards. Official railway company cards were published in thousands upon thousands. The most prolifically produced were those issued by the London & North Western Railway, and the most beautifully printed were those by McCorquodale and Raphael Tuck & Sons. But all the companies produced a variety of cards which usually started with the high-priced poster-type of advertisement postcards of maps, hotels, etc. Then there would be photographs of engines and rolling stock, followed by numerous series of views which would be overprinted by different railway companies. All of these cards are eagerly sought by collectors of today.

Raphael Tuck & Sons and the Locomotive Publishing Co. also concentrated upon publishing close-up views of railway engines, both standing in stations and puffing along at great speeds amidst clouds of steam. In the category of railway postcards, no detail or achievement of any company has been forgotten; narrow-gauge railways, electric-traction engines, underground railways, cliff-lifts and mountain railways, and official cards from every major and minor company ever to exist are to be found. But the most expensive cards to buy now are the ones featuring real photographic interiors of railway stations. As so many of these stations have disappeared or are no longer operating as stations, views of them on picture postcards are very often the only records which are left of their past glories. It is understandable then, that these cards should be at a premium. Even so, there are plenty of reasonably priced railway cards about, to tempt the beginner.

Religious postcards

People who lived in the Edwardian age were a much more God-fearing lot than most people today. While the majority of the religious cards embraced Christiantity – sets of 'The Lord's Prayer', 'The Ten Commandments', and the 'Stations of the Cross' being the firmest favourites to collect – there were also cards published which took into account the needs of other faiths.

But many of the religious cards publicized the activities of the various missionary societies, the portraits of clergymen, and the work of the Salvation Army. Roman Catholicism was also heavily featured with pictures of Popes, views of Lourdes and other places where miracles could be expected to take place. Exteriors and interiors of churches, cathedrals, and synagogues were photographed *ad infinitum* from every distance and from every angle, so prolifically produced were these particular postcards it might be wondered whether any other type of building ever existed.

Hymn cards were also produced by Bamforth's of Yorkshire, a sentimental picture on one portion of the card, the words and music score of the hymn on the other. 'Rock of Ages', Abide with me', 'The Old Rugged Cross', and 'Nearer, my God, to Thee', were among the most popular hymn titles. But the most poignant rendering of 'Nearer my God' appears on several cards which also show the sinking of the R.M.S. *Titanic*, the tragedy which stunned the world in 1912.

Romantic postcards

Bamforth & Co., Holmfirth, Yorkshire, also published literally thousands of sets of romantic song cards. Most of these were the sickly type of over-sentimental songs so beloved by Victorians, 'Sweet Genevieve', Sweet Adeline', 'Little Grey Home in the West', and 'Don't go down the Mine, Daddy' to name but a few. But to give some idea of the magnitude of the popularity the Bamforth song cards enjoyed, an American by the name of Major Robert W. Scherer of Florida produced three long check lists of the numbers and titles of the songs published. This labour of love is over one and a half inches thick, and is still not absolutely complete – for Major Scherer only included the coloured cards. Now he has passed the whole of his song-card collection into the custody of the Kirklees Libraries and Museum, Huddersfield.

Romantic postcards of the Edwardian era tended to come in sets of six, and mostly they were all photographic situations with titles such as, 'Love on a Balcony', 'Love under an Umbrella', 'Blossoming Romance', etc., etc. These sets usually followed the story from the first meeting until either a proposal was in the offing or a resounding slap across the face of the usually bewhiskered

Edwardian 'gentleman' who had leered his way through the whole set. Some of these cards are also screamingly funny – like the set which depicts a pair of would-be lovers courting on the bough of a tree over a pond, when, just as it looks as if he is to have his way, the bough breaks and down they go with a flurry of skirts and bloomers and trouser legs into the water below. Ardour thus cooled, the last card shows them walking off in different directions.

None of these cards is expensive, and there is a lot of fun to be had hunting for cards to complete the sets in this category.

Royalty postcards

Several long sets of the coronation processions of 1902 and 1911 were produced, and even longer ones of the funeral procession of Edward VII in 1910, so these cards are easy to find and extremely cheap to buy. Photographs of Royal visits and events are more difficult to come by, especially those which were photographed and printed privately.

The main interest in collecting Royalty postcards is centred round portraits of not only the British Royal family but the foreign royals as well, and the most keenly sought are those showing members of the Russian Royal family – especially informal photographs where glimpses of the infamous Rasputin is likely to be seen.

Raphael Tuck & Sons published many of the most desirable sets of Royalty themes, their 'Empire' series being one of the most delightful. Then there were sets to celebrate the coronations of Edward VII, and later George V; sets devoted completely to individual members of the British Royal family; and sets entitled 'The Belgian Royal House', and 'Unser Kronprinz'.

The splendour of coronation robes were further embellished by the use of 'jewels' – small pieces of sparkling paste used to highlight the crowns and regalia. Coronations were also the occasions when a number of firms snatched the opportunity to show their loyalty and to advertise their products at the same time: Horniman's Pure Tea offers 'A Right Royal Drink' to Edward VII by using trick photography to show the King holding a cup quite clearly marked 'Horniman's'; 'Weldon's Bazaar of Children's Fashions' presented a set of six Edward VII Souvenir postcards to their customers: Gossages superimposed the name of their soap on Royalty cards; and many firms over-printed their names and the nature of their products on the reverse sides of Coronation postcards.

Figure 13

Edward VII had earned a very special place in the hearts of the British people and when he died on 6 May 1910 there was a huge demand for the 'In Memoriam' cards that were published. The best known of these were produced by C. W. Faulkner who also printed at the same time Queen Alexandra's 'Letter to the Nation', dated 10 May 1910.

Royalty and other Heads of State were also the butts of more cruel pens, pencils, and pieces of charcoal! The French caricaturist, Rostro, lampooned every monarch of the 1903 period in his set entitled the 'Massacre of the Monarchs'. One of the examples showing what he thought of Edward VII is illustrated in Figure 13. Another French artist, Orens, displayed a similar harshness towards those with power and authority – including his version of Theodore Roosevelt, which could very well be captioned, 'Old money-bags, himself.' Mostly, however, postcards of royal personages are formal in their poses – that is until the Prince of Wales, who was later to become Edward VIII for a short period, brought an informal gaiety to the postcard world. His friendly waves and broad smiles immediately endeared him to the public, making people realize that Royalty were human like everyone else. Unquestionably, postcards portraying Royal families is a theme well worth a collection.

Shipping postcards

'Messing about with boats' has long been an international pastime, and for such devotees a collection of shipping postcards will not let them down. All the ships owned by the big merchant and passenger shipping lines appear on postcards, mostly photographed in close-up with details of tonnage, facilities for passengers, etc. And all the ships of the world's navies are equally well recorded. So are yachts and sailing events, barges progressing down the rivers, and the paddle-steamers crowded with starry-eyed passengers doubtlessly dreaming of the bigger adventure of sailing the seven seas.

The category of collecting shipping postcards is vast and yet one of the most complex of highly specialized subjects – as many a dealer has learned to his cost. Exploration of the wide, wide world started with sailing crafts, across the seas; fishermen cast nets into the water from simply contrived boats long before Christ captured the loyalty of James and Peter; the seamanship of war was foretold in the mythology of Jason and the Argonauts, centuries before the birth of Sir Francis Drake; and the elation of discovery was known to many seamen before Vasco da Gama discovered the Cape route to India and Christopher Columbus sighted America. The arts and traditions of seamanship are as deep and as noble as the sea itself – and yet, the humble picture postcard has managed to bring some of the awe and majesty of transport travelling the oceans to all who have the salt of the sea in their veins.

But not all collectors of shipping postcards are impelled by such an emotive excuse – there is another thraldom engendered by ship postmarks which collectors of postal history find difficult to resist; paquebot marks, 'posted on High Seas' marks, sea post-office marks, ship's cachets – and many other types of ship postmarks which are too esoteric for ordinary collectors of picture postcards to recognize. And, in addition, postal history collectors have discovered the rewarding pursuit of matching ships with ship postmarks which may be franked upon cards or other material that does not feature the names or pictures of the ships mentioned.

There is nothing light-hearted about building up a shipping collection – it is a deadly serious business, and unless new collectors have a true interest in the subject, and know what they are about, it is better for them to keep strictly to land-lubbing topics.

Sport on postcards

Be quite sure, wherever there is a ball to be seen being lobbed, kicked, thrown, or hit, there will be photographers breathlessly waiting to snap the dramas of whatever game is being played. The subject of sport is one of the rare categories of picture postcards where the rules and the fashions remain at a stand-still! True, the Edwardians had not reached the pitch when every goal scored turned the victorious side into a team of dancing bears, kissing and hugging whoever brought off such an amazing feat, but even so, the basic interest in ball games remains unchanged.

Baseball teams, football games, cricket matches, tennis tournaments, and golf competitions, each and every one had their fair share of the limelight focused on postcards. Athletics, boxing, swimming, rowing, wrestling, gymnastics, bullfighting, mountaineering, hunting, fishing, and shooting, did not do so badly either. The stars of every sport were photographed both in closeup and in action; football, rugby, and cricket grounds (and their pavilions) were photographed with monotonous regularity – so were tennis courts, golf links, boxing rings, and gymnasiums.

Race-courses, all the classic races to be run on them, and all the famous jockeys up on the winning horses became certain post-card favourites with the race-going fraternity. And the postcards which colourfully featured blood sports were not squeamish about following the hunt to the bitter end. Hunting and bullfight-ing cards are not now as popular as they were – judging by the numbers to be seen lingering and languishing on the shelves of dealers, and most of the other sporting subjects are in short supply, but with a little patience examples of most sporting subjects can still be found.

Theatrical postcards

An hour or so with a collection of early theatrical action stills of Edwardian plays, music-hall acts, ballet, and opera scenes, has made many of today's collectors wistful for the days when enter-tainment was something meant to be enjoyed. Postcards of the great Edwardian artistes of the theatres and music-halls of those days were excitements to be collected by everyone. No album was complete without several cards of Gladys Cooper, Marie Studholme, the Dare sisters, and Camille Clifford; Henry Irving, Beerbohm Tree, Oscar Asche, and Henry Ainley, to mention just a fraction of the long list of names which would fill a book on its own!

J. Beagles & Co., London, and the Rotary Photo Co., London, were the main publishing firms to specialize in photographing theatrical personalities, and such was their popularity that literally thousands of examples can still be found today – mostly for a few pence, unless, of course, they are autographed, when the pence required will very quickly change into pounds!

Nights spent at the opera, the ballet, or the play were not to be compared with the robust jollity of the music-hall where stars such as Albert Chevalier, Gaby Deslys, Vesta Tilley, and Marie Lloyd played to packed houses. Postcards of artistes like these im-mediately conjure up visions of the gilt and plush of music-hall theatres, and the atmosphere generated by audiences noisily waiting to be entertained – and woe-betide the 'turn' who failed to come up to scratch! Music-halls were not the places where polite applause could be accepted by performers as the hall-mark of approval; applause had to be deafening and accompanied by cheering shouts for encores. Music-halls were spell binding places where the wishes of audiences were the performer's command, places where tensions relaxed and pressures lifted, places where people could let their hair down and get on with the fun of simply enjoying themselves. The close proximity of a thousand people sharing the same warmth, joining in the songs, crying with laughter, cheering – and jeering – and urging the high-kicking beauties to kick just that bit higher. How can the drear of the bingo hall, the echo of bowling alleys, or the cold impersonal screen of the television set make up for the companionship offered by a visit to the music-hall?

Much of the gaiety of the music-hall and the lighter play productions was promoted on postcard by play-bill advertising posters. The best of these were produced by David Allen who frequently used some of the top artists of the day such as Tom Browne, John Hassall, and Lance Thackeray to draw scenes from shows. Postcards such as these would mainly be sold in the foyers of the theatres, and of course they were immediately popular with theatre-goers who more than probably formed the habit of buying one for themselves and several to send to their friends. Then there were the very scarce Barnum & Bailey, and Buffalo Bill's Wild West Show poster cards which were produced in such limited editions; it is hardly fair to mention them.

Bringing on the clowns was a favourite theme of early postcard publishers, as were most circus acts. Concert parties, pierrots, escapologists, and performing animals were also eagerly collected by the Edwardian public. In fact, the picture postcard captures the essence of all the heady scents of show-business; the grease-paint of the actors, the perfumes of the audience, the smell of the animals being led into the circus ring, and, yes, the odours of nervous tension, too! The performers of Edwardian show-business? The picture postcard did them proud!

Transport postcards

Wheels in Edwardian times were mostly horse-drawn. The bells of fire-engines would be accompanied by a clatter of hooves as they sped over the cobbled streets of the towns and cities, and so were the ambulances. Motorized *public* transport did not become generally accepted as convenient conveyances until about the middle of the First World War, a period which is beyond the confines of this book. But the Wolseley Car Company supplied a few 18 h.p. Siddeley vehicles fitted as ambulances to some of the major British cities between 1906 and 1907, some of which have appeared on postcards.

There are also a few scarce postcards around showing the first Daimler car ordered by Edward VII in 1900 – but as the German firm of Daimler had been operating since 1893 there are doubtless a number of postcards showing cousin William, the Kaiser, boasting a Daimler or two.

By 1910, there were a few smallish motor-buses to be seen on postcards, but by then most towns and cities had only just become accustomed to the new electrified tram system in Britain. And now that both the horse-drawn transport and almost all the trams with their tram lines have disappeared, all cards featuring these modes of travel are exceedingly popular.

But, generally, anything to be seen on wheels on a postcard between 1900 and 1914 usually has a high price-tag attached. After 1914, photographic postcards of motorized vehicles gradually became more common.

So from the brief outlines of the major categories of postcards we have listed here, some gauge of the enormous variety of early postcards will be seen. In fact, such was that variety, that dealers today never cease to be surprised – for even though they may have seen and handled a million postcards in their time, in almost every new collection to come their way they will find at least one example which has hitherto been unknown to them. This constant element of surprise is one of the greatest charms of collecting picture postcards, for while there are many collectors of specialized subjects who are highly regarded as experts – no one yet has dared to make the claim of being omniscient!

Newcomers, then, can enter the field of collecting picture postcards and start enjoying themselves from the beginning with only one maxim to remember, and that is, 'collect what you like, enjoy what you collect – and let the investment angle look after itself'. It will!

4 *A Postcard Miscellany*

Once collectors have been bitten by the postcard-collecting bug, it is not long before they begin to ask where check lists and other information can be found about their own particular interests. Complete check lists of any subject are difficult to find, and even if they were readily available it would be impossible to include them in this book. We can, however, supplement our thematic chapter by giving a short summary of some of the more important titles, sets and series which were published, and a list of the names and whereabouts of postcard clubs and the specialist collectors who are able to give further information and advice.

Art Nouveau

French types – examples by Raphael Kirchner, Viennese artist (1876–1917).

La Jolie Maud	Rose respirant une Femme	Le masque impassible
La premier violette	Delicious Fruits	Enfants de la Mer
Greek Maidens	Les Pêches Capitaux	Demi-Vierges
Flirtation	Danseuse de Montmatre	Silhouette de Montmatre
San Toy	Mikado	Geisha

| Skating Girls | Lelie, fumeuse d'opium | Le coup de la Jarretelle |
| Marionettes | Sun Rays | The Harem |

Bruton Street Gallery types of more moderately priced Kirchner examples.

Bubbles	Harlequinade	Miss Red Cap
Merci	Cupid's Captive	Rosalba
Lolotte	Stop	The Fan

Plus many, many more titles.

Alphonse Mucha – Czech artist (1860–1939).

Job Cigarettes	Moët & Chandon	The Four Seasons
La Plume	The Four Flowers	The Twelve Months of the Year
Ideal Heads	Chansons d'aïeuls	Femme au Chevalet
Touha à Laska	Fleur de Cerisier	The Four Times of Day
Primevére	The Four Stars	Nectar
Zodiac	Nestlé's Food	The Four Precious Stones
Gismonda	La Dame aux Camélias	

Plus many more.

Eugène Grasset – Swiss artist (1841–1917).

| Sarah Bernhardt | Tinta L. Marquet | Salon des cent |

Eugène Grasset either signed his name Grasset with the 'E' enclosed within the 'G', or he used his initials 'G' enclosing 'E' against the last letter 'T' of his name.

Paul Berthon – Swiss artist, and pupil of Grasset (1872–1909).

| La Viole de gambe | La Vague | L'Ermitage La Maddore, Le Violon |

to name a few examples.

Georges de Feure – French artist (1868–1943).

Retour	Octave Uzanne	Le Journal des Ventes

Very rare and very expensive!

Annie French – Scottish artist (1872–1965).
Specialized in Art Nouveau themes based on nursery rhymes – and so did ...

Jessie M. King – also a Scottish artist (1876–1949).

Felix Vallotton – Swiss artist (1865–1935).
Mainly produced black and white Art Nouveau engravings.

William H. Bradley – American artist (1868–1962).

The Skirt Dancer	When Hearts are Trumps	Masquerade

A few examples of the postcards published by Raphael Tuck & Sons

Kings and Queens of England – *Series Nos 614, 615, and 616.*

1st Series, Nos 1–12	2nd Series, Nos 13–24	3rd Series, Nos 25–36
William I	Henry IV	Charles I
William II	Henry V	Oliver Cromwell
Henry I	Henry VI	Charles II
Stephen	Edward IV	James II
Henry II	Edward V	William & Mary
Richard I	Richard III	Anne
John	Henry VII	George I
Henry III	Henry VIII	George II
Edward I	Edward VI	George III
Edward II	Mary	George IV
Edward III	Elizabeth I	William IV
Richard II	James I	Victoria

This set was completed with card No 617 of Edward VII – of which there are several variants.

Some titles and numbers of series of Tuck's 'In Dickens Land': Nos 6012 and 6046, 'Pickwick Papers'; 6047 & 6048, 'David Copperfield'; 6050 & 7060, 'Dombey & Son'; 6051, 'Bleak House'; 6052, 'Nicholas Nickleby'; 7058, 'Martin Chuzzlewit'; 7059, 'Little Dorrit'; and 9852, 'Character Sketches from Dickens' by Harold Copping. There are many more sets to be added to the 'In Dickens Land' series.

Cupid's Alphabet – Series No 6114. A beautifully embossed and coloured set of twenty-six cards – slightly in the Art Nouveau class.

Zodiac – Series No 128. Early Tuck's set of twelve cards drawn by Dwig, illustrating the months of the year with zodiac signs.

'Name' – Series No 131. One of the seemingly endless sets of 'first names' written in large script surrounded by suitable embellishments. No one quite knows how many of this series were published.

'Celebrated Posters'. The beautiful poster-type advertisements produced by Tuck's for firms such as Fry's, Dewars' Whisky, Hoe's Sauce, Ogden's Cigarettes, Cadbury's, Milkmaid, and Pear's – to mention a few of the firms publicized on the seventy-two cards which were issued. The series numbers of each set of six started from 1500.

'Wagner' series-numbered from 690 to 695. Portrays scenes from Wagner's operas and boast distinctly Art Nouveau borders.

But the firm of Raphael Tuck & Sons produced such a wealth of postcards in almost infinite variety, the task of describing and hopefully listing them all would be the most daunting enterprise.

Mrs Sally S. Carver has already produced the excellent book, *The American Postcard Guide to TUCK's*, and in Britain, Mr Tony Warr is devoting all his spare time to producing a definitive work on the postcards produced by this most fabulous firm. Even so, our book will not be complete without mention of some of the very scarce series published by Tuck's.

Sets like series Nos 810–815 which feature superbly coloured, gilded and embossed pictures of British politicians with similar

"PHIL MAY" POST CARDS.

But three sets of Post Cards, six subjects to each set, have ever been specially designed by this great English humorist, the commission having been placed by us shortly before his lamented demise.

PROOFS.

A limited edition of 1000 SETS of PROOFS of each of these three series, each set being numbered and placed in a suitable portfolio, is being issued by us at the price of 5s. each set, every purchaser of a Proof Set having his name registered as the owner.

A POPULAR EDITION OF THESE "PHIL MAY"
POST CARDS

is also issued at the price of 6d. each set of six; both editions may be procured from all the leading Stationers, Booksellers, and Art Dealers throughout the world.

OUR OTHER "QUAINT" AND "HUMOROUS"
SERIES OF POST CARDS

comprise designs by the leading Artists of the day, among whom are LANCE THACKERAY, CECIL ALDIN, LOUIS WAIN, HILDA COWHAM, JOHN HASSALL, TOM BROWNE, PERCY BRADSHAW, WILL OWEN, GUNNING KING, EDWARD KING, DUDLEY HARDY, etc. etc.; our arrangements with many of these Artists *confining their work for Post Cards entirely to our firm.*

A "*VANITY FAIR*" series of Post Cards is being issued by us by special arrangement with the proprietors of "Vanity Fair."

Our complete Post Card List, including our famous "OILETTE" VIEW SERIES, "PLAY PICTORIAL" SERIES, and a host of other varieties, comprising upwards of 10,000 subjects, is supplied free by all Post Card Dealers.

Raphael, Tuck & Sons Ltd.,

Art Publishers to Their Majesties The King and Queen, and Their Royal Highnesses The Prince and Princess of Wales,

RAPHAEL HOUSE, MOORFIELDS, CITY, LONDON.
THE ACKNOWLEDGED PIONEERS OF PICTURE POST CARDS.

Figure 14. Raphael Tuck advertisement.

series published of British generals; the Connoisseur 'Empire' series, No 2558, of embossed monograms of noble British orders; and the lovely chromographed series, No 6087, 'For England, Home & Beauty' by Harry Payne. Then there are the gorgeous vignettes of the 'Sport' series, No 512, the embossed sets for 'St Patrick's Day,' and the umpteen early sets to celebrate the American Thanksgiving.

Raphael Tuck & Sons were also the only firm to produce limited editions of proof sets of postcards, and as can be seen from a copy of one of their advertisements, reproduced opposite, Tuck's published the work of many other artists in their proof editions, as well as the fine drawings by Phil May. Phil May died at the age of thirty-nine in August 1903, and although a number of reproductions of his work appears on postcards, only the three sets commissioned by Tuck's were designed especially for postcards.

Two other sparkling ideas to stimulate the picture-postcard-collecting hobby also came from Tuck's – the introduction of Exchange Clubs and Prize Competitions. Every year they produced a 'Postcard Exchange Register' which listed the names of some '2,000 ladies and gentlemen in every part of the world, who will exchange Tuck's postcards with you. Details of this club, and

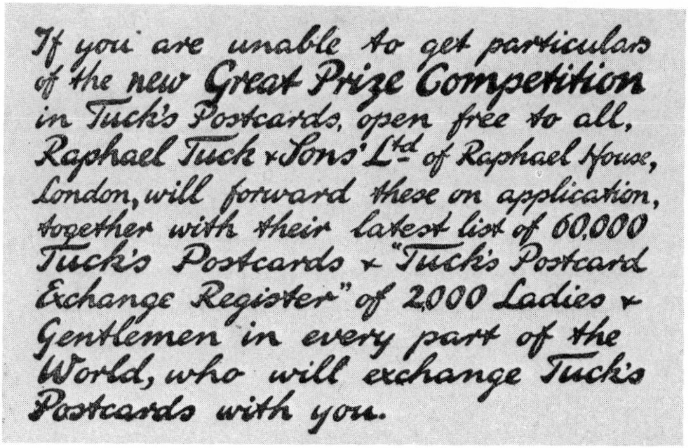

If you are unable to get particulars of the new Great Prize Competition in Tuck's Postcards, open free to all, Raphael Tuck & Sons' Ltd of Raphael House, London, will forward these on application, together with their latest list of 60,000 Tuck's Postcards & "Tuck's Postcard Exchange Register" of 2000 Ladies & Gentlemen in every part of the World, who will exchange Tuck's Postcards with you.

Figure 15. Prize Competition.

how early collectors of Tuck's postcards could get particulars of the 'Great Prize Competitions' are shown in the small blurb on the previous page. These tiny leaflets were inserted with the sets of postcards sold in packets.

A variety of comic artists and their series

Tom Browne examples published by Davidson Bros.

The Amateur Photographer	The Pierrots	Yeomanry
Cycling	Home Sweet Home	Japanese Humour
How Jim Took Exercise	In Lodgings	A Thing of the Past, Old Dear
Out on the Deep	Seaside	Popular Songs Illustrated
Honeymoon	Spooning	Illustrated Sports
Poor Pa's Troubles	Uncle Podger	Illustrated Bridge

Plus many more sets of human situations.

Fred Buchanan – mainly published by Tuck's in their Oilette series.

News Bulletins, No 3620	All Scotch	Stock Exchange Items, No 3615
Wireless News, No 3618	Gardening Hints	Football Illustrated, No 3623
Proverbs Illustrated	Unsolicited Testimonials, etc., etc.	

Percy V. Bradshaw – whose postcards are now eagerly sought by today's collectors (Tuck's Series).

The Cockney Yachtsman, No 1768	Market Reports, No 1001	Billiard Terms, No 1288
Racing Illustrated, No 1178		

are a few examples of the sets by this accomplished artist.

94

Dudley Hardy examples published by Davidson Bros.

Why Smith Left Home	A Horse, a Horse, My Kingdom for a Horse!
Some Day	You Must call the Lady, Mother!
Oft in the Stilly Night	Japhet in Search of a Father!
The Medal & the Maid	Persuasion is Better than Force.

Dudley Hardy also produced a number of sketches for poster-type advertisements, and so did –

John Hassall – another of the favourite comic artists. Examples of his work includes many sets such as the 'Illustrated Poems', and the 'Illustrated Proverbs' series.

Louis Wain

The man who filled thousands of sketch-books with his drawings of animals, birds, and frogs cavorting about in human situations produced his scrupulously detailed work for French and German publishers as well as for over thirty British postcard manufacturers. Up until the beginning of the First World War, Louis Wain was one of the most industrious artists, whose work was enormously admired by everybody who saw it. Unfortunately, he had no head for business, for when he sold his drawings, the copyright for reproducing them *ad infinitum* was included in his fee. In 1923, this brilliant man ended up in the paupers' ward of a Metropolitan asylum where he stayed until a report in the London *Times* in 1925 revealed his plight and announced that an appeal was being launched to get him into a private hospital.

A souvenir of Louis Wain's work was published in which the plea by Mrs Cecil Chesterton was reprinted from the September 1925 edition of *Animals* magazine.

'Louis Wain [said Mrs Chesterton] is in a pauper lunatic asylum. This must come as a great shock to the many thousands who have loved and admired his work. For years Louis Wain

95

cats decorated our hoardings, adorned the covers of our magazines and were familiarly loved by every child and the majority of grown-ups. No Christmas calendar was complete without this artist, no annual was issued that did not contain one of his vivid sketches.' [And the same could have been said about postcard albums! But to continue]:

'And yet, at the age of 65, he is so bereft of means that in his affliction, he is compelled to accept the hospitality of a State institution. How has this come about? It is not a story of extravagance or heedlessness. Louis Wain was not one of those men who took no thought for the morrow. For years this artist made a fair income. But with a lack of business acumen, so often allied to genius, when he sold his drawings he parted with them outright.'

The plea went on to describe the intense privation, mental strain, and bewilderment which precipitated the breakdown of Louis Wain. But the compassionate result of the appeal allowed him to be transferred to Napsbury Hospital, near St Albans, where he remained until he died in 1939.

Now, as with the paintings of famous artists, who seemed traditionally to die in poverty, which fetch huge sums at auction, Louis Wain postcards have also reached the double-figure bracket.

The descriptions of postcards just mentioned represent the merest fraction of the array published between 1894 and 1914. A broader range appears in the section headed, 'A Quick Guide to Postcards'.

Postcard Clubs and Specialist Collectors

BRITISH CLUBS
The Postcard Club of Great Britain,
Mrs Drene Brennan, 34 Harper House, St James's Crescent, Brixton, London SW9 7DW, England.

The Norfolk Postcard Club,
Mr P. J. Standley, 63 Folly Road, Wymondham, Norfolk, England.

Huddersfield & District Postcard Society,
Mr George Wolstenholme, 13 Westroyd Park, Mirfield, West Yorkshire, England.

Mercia Postcard Club,
Mr Maurice L. Palmer, 5 Saxon Rise, Earls Barton, Northampton, England.

Bradford & District Postcard Society,
Mr A. E. Wood, 26 Front View, Shelf, Halifax, Yorkshire, England.

Avon Postcard Club,
Mrs M. Freeman, 24 Cherry Orchard, Pershore, Worcestershire, England.

London Postcard Club,
Mrs Joyce Cohen, 58 Sandringham Road, London N.W.11, England.

Tuck's Collectors Circle,
Mr David Pinfold, 7 Glenville, Northampton NN3 1LZ, England.

UNITED STATES POSTCARD CLUBS

The Sunshine Postcard Club,
Mrs Alberta Worland, 120 Park Avenue, Satellite Beach, Florida, U.S.A.

Golden Gate Postcard Club,
Mr Arthur Chase, 4150 Folsom, San Francisco, California, U.S.A.

The Garden State Postcard Club,
Mr Chriss Wolff, 44 Beech Avenue, Berkeley Heights, New Jersey, U.S.A.

Metropolitan Postcard Collectors of New York,
Mr J. Nardone, 323 E. Gunhill Road, Apartment 2A, Bronx, New York, U.S.A.

The Santa Monica Postcard Club,
Mr Adrian Verburg, 1112 11th Street, Santa Monica, California, U.S.A.

The Monument Postcard Club,
Mr Roland Tankersley, 5007 Fleetwood Avenue, Baltimore, Ohio, U.S.A.

For further information about American postcard clubs, write to Roy and Marilyn Nuhn, editors of, *The American Postcard Journal*, Box 562, West Haven, Connecticut, U.S.A.

Specialist Collectors who are Prepared to Help and Advise New Collectors

Art Nouveau	Mr Bill Varnham, 21 Tranquil Vale, Blackheath, London S.E.3, London, England.
Aviation	Mr Francis Field, 10 Richmond Road, Sutton Coldfield, West Midlands, England.
Advertising	Mr Ken Lawson, 24 Watford Road, Wembley HA0 3EP. Middlesex, England.
Children	Mr Peter Cope, 12 Camden Row, Blackheath, London S.E.3, England.

Comic	Mr Ken Lawson, 24 Watford Road, Wembley HA0 3EP, Middlesex, England – for information on Tom Browne. Mr Rex Needle, 31 Lincoln Road, Northborough, Peterborough PE6 9BL, England – for information on Lawson Wood. Mr David Pearlman, 36 Asmuns Hill, London N.W.11, England – for information on Phil May, Dudley Hardy, Lance Thackeray, and many other comic artists.
Exhibitions	Mr Chris Morrison, 65 Rothesay Avenue, Greenford, Middlesex, England.
Grüss aus	Mr Ken Lake, 106 Bedford Chambers, Covent Garden, London, England.
Louis Wain	Mr C. W. E. Coles, 103 Alcester Road South, Birmingham 14, England.
Military	Mr Jack Duke, 5 Weavill's Road, Bishopstoke, Eastleigh, Hampshire, England.
Novelty	Mr Malcolm Hughes, 13 Tagwell Road, Droitwich Spa, Worcestershire, England.
Publishers	Mr A. Byatt, 28 St Peter's Road, Malvern, Worcestershire, England.
Railway	Mr John Silvester, 49 Barn Hill, Wembley Park, Middlesex, England.
R. Phillimore & S. Endacott	Mrs Joan Humphreys, 5 Eagley Bank, Shawforth, Whitworth, Rochdale, Lancashire, England.
Shipping	Mr C. W. E. Coles, 103 Alcester Road South, Birmingham 14, England.

99

Theatre	Mr John Hall, 17 Harrington Road, South Kensington, London S.W.7, England.
Woven and Embroidered Silk cards	Mr C. Radley, 22 Longreach Court, King Edward's Road, Barking, Essex, England.
J. Welch & Sons, Portsmouth	Dr Charles W. Hollingsworth, 17 Mellish Road, Walsall, Staffordshire, England. Welch cards not only include views but also the 'Language' series of postcards, e.g. Flowers. Vegetables, etc.
Horse racing	Mr Nick Pugh, Pinnerwood Lodge, Woodhall Road, Pinner, Middlesex, England.
Fantasy	Mr Dave Brooks, 56 Castle Road, Epsom, Surrey, England.
Tuck's cards	Mr Tony Warr, Fairview, Ickford Road, Shabbington, Aylesbury, Buckinghamshire, England. Mr Warr is also the founder of the 'Study Circle for Early Numbered Tuck' postcards – membership FREE – apart from the enclosures of the usual s.a.e.
Postmarks – Canadian & GB Squared Circles	Mr Stanley Cohen, 51 Westfield Road, Edgbaston, Birmingham 15, England.
Postmarks – General & GB Duplex	Mr Maurice Hewlett, The Hermitage, Box, nr Corsham, Wiltshire, England.

How to store postcard collections

The curious question about when the first postcard albums appeared was answered by Mr Peter Lawrence – one of Britain's most knowledgeable collectors of all kinds of Victorian ephemera, including postcards. His records show that Stanley Gibbons advertised in 1888, 'The Imperial Post Card Album' in four styles priced from 3s to 3s 6d; in 1894, W. G. Schäffels Albumfabrik, Leipzig, specialized in the production of postcard albums – and won a prize for the best produced at the 1898 Munich Exhibition, 'Postkarten-Album-Ausstellung'; and another firm of English stamp-dealers, Lincoln, William & Simpson, were manufacturing albums specifically designed for postcards by 1896.

The earliest reference to an album written on a postcard is dated 22 December 1896. This card also belongs to Mr Peter Lawrence, and comes from the greatest postcard collection ever made, the 'Royal Collection' of Princess Gerta-Wilhelm of Saxe Weimar which extended from 1896 to 1941!

To find an early album in fine condition today – especially the fine example owned by Mr Frank Staff which is free-standing and gives almost a three-dimensional effect to the cards it displays – is becoming increasingly rare. But even when old albums in reasonable condition are found, modern collectors are reluctant to use them. Early postcards which have mellowed with age have also become frail at the corners, and attempting to slot them into early albums can be an infuriating business. So most albums now are the ones with plastic pockets in which postcards can be easily inserted. Prices for these vary from about £2 up to £12 for the very large types. Obviously albums are the most convenient way in which postcards can be stored and the sight of them enjoyed to the full. But ordinary boxes similar to stationery or shoeboxes are frequently used by people who prefer to spend their available cash on buying cards rather than on albums, and quantities of Cellophane or plastic bags of postcard size can be bought very reasonably for the purpose of protecting cards housed in boxes.

Ordinary scrapbooks which can be purchased from most stationers shops have also been put to good use by some of the more enterprising collectors. Armed with scrapbooks and a supply of adhesive photographic corners, collections can be arranged to suit the tastes and requirements of the collector without having to bother about whether cards are of the vertical type or the horizontal kind; for most collectors know about the frustrations of finding sets with a mixture of the two.

A cautionary word in the ears of collectors who use plastic bags or albums with plastic pockets will, we hope, not be amiss – DO take cards out of these containers occasionally, to allow them to 'breathe', otherwise fox marks and other disagreeable blemishes might appear.

Fakes, forgeries, and reprints

And here is another cautionary tale. Recently a collector blissfully remarked, 'At least we don't get many faked or forged cards, like stamps!' Do we not?

In the days when postcards could be had for 'two a penny' there would be no point in faking or forging them. It is a different story now. Postcards have been recognized as pasteboard antiques – some of which are quite valuable, and value usually implies money. So as jolting as it may sound, the industry of faking, forging, and reprinting early postcards does exist. Faked cards deliberately prepared to deceive. Forged cards fraudulently imitating the earlier versions. Reprinted cards giving new impressions of early issues – often quite innocently without any thought to dupe prospective purchasers. Newcomers to postcard collecting, and indeed the more advanced collectors, should be wary of all three of these odd classifications, especially now that so many of the early cards are beginning to command high catalogue prices. It has been known for faked and forged cards – and some of the reprints – to be sold as genuine.

How can intentional attempts to mislead be avoided? The simple answer, of course, is to advise collectors to buy only those cards which have been through the post, complete with the appropriate stamps and postmarks. But this will not suit collectors who prefer their cards to be in mint condition, nor will it deter the activities of faked card makers – as the first of the short guides will show!

Faked cards are comparatively easy to contrive. The method is to split early postally used postcards of the less important variety in two, either by soaking in water or using a sharp blade. Then on the reverse side of the postally used part, a reprint of some merit is pasted, thus at a quick glance a 'good' card purporting to have hailed from the right era by virtue of the postmark is shown. In fact, some people have used this method to transfer mint backs bearing the $\frac{1}{2}$d postage rate on to modern reprints. So, apart from *Panel* cards which are naturally 'heavy-weight', postcards which appear abnormally *thick* should be examined for *joins* at the edges – especially if there is some doubt that the picture side does not appear to correspond with the era of the postal side!

Forged postcards are quite a different proposition. Apart from the laws of copyright, there is the common law which requires the printer to publish the name and address of the publisher either on the front or the reverse side of postcards. When reprints are intended deliberately to deceive, this information is either omitted, or worse, the facsimiles of the original publishers appear where they would normally be found. But somewhere along the line the idea of making money will be a prime factor in forging operations, and, for such ventures to be profitable, forged post-cards would have to be produced in sufficient quantity to make the effort worthwhile. Even so, it does no harm for dealers and collectors alike to keep a look-out for hitherto 'rare' cards sud-denly being offered in suspiciously large quantities – perhaps under the guise of ex-stationers' stock fortuitously discovered in a building which has 'since been demolished'!

As the prices of the genuinely early postcards continue to rise as they become scarcer to find, more and more of them will appear as reprints. And as long as the word, 'reprint' or 'reproduction' appears somewhere on these cards, together with details of the new publishers, collectors could be grateful for such an enterprise. But it must be mentioned that there are some excellent reprints in existence today which were produced on the continent and originally sold as 'nostalgia' postcards for a few pence each, which are so good they could now be taken for the 'real thing', and priced accordingly.

Fortunately, all the reputable postcard dealers are wide-awake to such tricks, but it is as well to warn those who are less experi-enced, and to give some guide-lines on how to avoid the traps!

5 *Notes on Colour Plates*

When the illustrations in the colour section were first published as postcards their average cost was a penny apiece. The value of many of them has now risen by several thousand per cent. It is impossible, therefore, for us to be categoric about current and future values; we can only give some idea of rarity factors. This we do by using a series of asterisks which will, in the event of evaluating rare cards, be combined with the letter R. The guide to the use of this arrangement is:

*   represents the lowest valuation for postcards judged to be plentiful;
**   for cards bordering on specialized categories;
***   specialized cards in limited supply;
****R demand well exceeding the supply;
RRR   almost impossible to find and *very* expensive when they are.

As the years go by, of course, some of the lowest priced postcards will find themselves promoted into the higher brackets, and many others will be labelled with the triple rarity factor RRR.

Plate 1 – Early undivided back published by A. C. Bosselman & Co., New York, printed in Germany. Category: American topographical. Value *.

Plate 2 – 'Cosmopolitan New York', vegetable stands, 'Little Italy'. Tuck's Oilette No. 1738, postmarked 1905. Category: American Tuck's. Value **.

Plate 3 – The Obelisk, Central Park, New York, drawn by Charles E. Flower. From the Raphael Tuck *Wide Wide World* series 'New York', Oilette No 7245. Category: American, artistic topographical. Value **.

Plate 4 – Artist-drawn street scene, published and printed in America. Category: American topographical. Value *.

Plate 5 – Photographic view of the Vor dem Hotel, Lucerne, Switzerland. Published and printed in Zürich. Category: Swiss topographical. Value *.

Plate 6 – The Royal Exchange and Bank of England Published by the *Rapid Photo Printing Co.*, London. Category: British topographical. Value *.

Plate 7 – Parisian view of Tour St Jaques, Paris. Published and printed in France. Early undivided back, postmarked 1902. Category: French topographical. Value *.

Plate 8 – American 'Grüss aus' type of 'Private Mailing Card'. Published by Carson-Harper Co., Denver, postmarked 1904. Category: special American topographical. Value ***.

Plate 9 – Photographed and published by the Neurdein Bros. Category: French topographical. Value *.

Plate 10 – A typical specimen of an early German 'Grüss aus' postcard. Multi-vignettes of Offenburg. Published by K. Hagen, Offenburg. Categories: German topographical and specialist 'Grüss aus'. Value ***.

Plate 11 – Triple vignette 'Grüss aus' postcard of Marienbad. Published by Hermann Seibt, Meissen. Category: early German topographical – but since World War II and the change of name to Marianske Lazne, Marienbad cards can now be found under Czechoslovakian topography as well. Value ***.

Plate 12 – Moonlight impression of the Berlin Opera House by J. Miesler. Dated 1900, and published and printed in Germany. Category: artist-drawn German topography. Value ***.

Plate 13 – Early undivided back, postmarked 1903. Published and printed in France. Categories: French topographical and early French transport. Value ∗∗.

Plate 14 – Interior of the restaurant of the Hotel Cecil, London – a favourite haunt of Edwardian sophisticates. Publisher and printer unknown – but was probably an advertising card for the hotel. Categories: advertising and interiors. Value ∗∗.

Plate 15 – The lounge of the Durley Dene Hotel, Bournemouth, drawn by 'Jotter', and published by the hotel management. Categories: advertising and interiors. Value ∗∗.

Plate 16 – Another hotel interior showing the enormous proportions of the Liverpool Street Hotel dining-room. Publisher and printer unknown. Categories: advertising, interiors, and railway. Value ∗∗.

Plate 17 – Interior of the dining-room of the Rougemont Hotel, Exeter. Publisher and printer unknown. Categories: advertising and interiors. Value ∗∗.

Plate 18 – Exterior of the Grosvenor Hotel, adjoining London's Victoria Station – where Mrs Joan Venman and Mr Ron Meade pioneered the ventures of the craze for postcard fairs in the second Elizabethan age. Published by Pitman's of London. Categories: advertising and railway. Value ∗∗.

Plate 19 – The 'Costume Salon at Harrods of London' published as an unnumbered oilette by Raphael Tuck & Sons. Categories: advertising and interiors. Value ∗∗∗.

Plate 20 – Advertisement card for Churchill's, the famous club and restaurant on Broadway and FortyNinth Street, New York – the name of which was probably induced by the marriage of Randolph Churchill to Jenny, one of the most ravishing beauties of American and British Society in Edwardian times. Published in America by the Souvenir Post Card Co., N.Y. Categories: American advertising and interiors. Value ∗∗. (A special feature of the reverse side of this card is the invitation that 'We furnish the stamp'!)

Plate 21 – A 'Correspondence Card' issued by Frascati's of London. Category: advertising and interiors. Value ∗∗.

Plate 22 – Another unnumbered example published by Tuck's

from their 'London Coliseum' series. Categories: theatre advertising and interiors. Value **.

Plate 23 – Dancing in the Ballroom at the Zoological Gardens, Belle Vue, Manchester. Published by Horrocks & Co. Categories: advertising and interiors. Value **.

Plate 24 – Hook & ladder Truck No. 1, going to a fire, Providence, Rhode Island. Published by S.L. & Co., U.S.A. Categories: American topographical and fire transport. Value ***.

Plate 25 – Heavily embossed and coloured full-out side crest of the coat-of-arms of the city of Chester, England. Published by the Rapid Photo Printing Co., London. Category: heraldic. Value **.

Plate 26 – From 'Fighting the Flames' series, Oilette No. 6459, published by Tuck's. Category: fires. Value ***.

Plate 27 – Example of a Ja-Ja centrally placed crest of the coat-of-arms of the Borough of Paddington, London. Category: heraldic. Value **.

Plate 28 – Silver-backed example of a 'glow-card' showing the 'Palace of Electricity' at the World's Fair, St Louis, 1904 (A glow-card is a form of hold-to-light, which when held to artificial lamplight the coloured parts of the card glow against the darkened backgrounds of silver, gold, and black! Produced by Samuel Cupples Envelope Co., St Louis. Categories: exhibition and novelty. Value ***.

Plate 29 – Official picture postcard commemorating the World's Columbian Exposition, Chicago, 1893. The example here bears two British 1893 postmarks which puts this card into the class of being ****R – had it been franked with the official exhibition mark it would have been classed as RRR! Category: important early exhibitions. Value ****R.

Plate 30 – Interior of a Monte Carlo gaming-room, photographed by Giletta of Nice and published and printed in France. Categories: gambling or gaming. Value **.

Plate 31 – A superb embossed and gilded Souvenir de Monte Carlo card with Art Nouveau embellishments. Early undivided back, published and printed in France. Categories: gambling, coinage, playing card themes. Value RRR.

Plate 32 – Another Souvenir de Monte Carlo card inviting the illustrious and the infamous to 'place their bets'. Early undivided back, published by Guggenheim & Co., Zurich. Category: gambling. Value ***.

Plate 33 – Early undivided back example showing the Town Hall, Basle, Switzerland. Published by Glockner–Blattman. Category: Swiss topography. Value *.

Plate 34 – The Curtiss biplane, from the 'Famous Aeroplanes' Oilette No. 9943, published by Raphael Tuck & Sons. Category: Aviation. Value ****R.

Plate 35 – A drawing by Hans Rudolf Schulze showing a Zeppelin over the English countryside. An early World War I propaganda postcard with German field post office marks on the reverse side. Categories: aviation and W.W.I propaganda. Value ****R.

Plate 36 – One of the 'Military in London' series published by Tuck's. Oilette No. 3546E drawn by Harry Payne. Category: military. Value ***.

Plate 37 – One of the superimposed dirigibles about to pass over the Eiffel Tower. Printed and published in France. Categories: French topographical and aviation. Value ***.

Plate 38 – Another military postcard drawn by Harry Payne from 'Our Fighting Regiments' series, Oilette No. 3165, published by Tuck's. Category: military. Value ***.

Plate 39 – The Grenadier Guards at Wellington Barracks, by Harry Payne, from the 'Military in London', series No. 3546C, published by Tuck's. Category: military. Value ***.

Plate 40 – Drawing by R. Caton-Woodville of the Russian retreat after Kiu-lien-cheng, during the Russo-Japanese war. Published by Valentine & Son, England. Categories: military & Russo-Japanese. Value ****R.

Plate 41 – 'The Rifle Brigade' drawn by Edgar A. Holloway. Published by Gale & Polden, Aldershot. Category: military. Value ***.

Plate 42 – Reconnoitering patrol of the Argyll & Sutherland

Highlanders, by Harry Payne. Oilette No. 9937, published by Tuck's. Category: military. Value ✱✱✱.

Plate 43 – Royal Engineers (officer cadets) on manœuvres. Published by Max Ettlinger & Co. from the 'Life in the Army' series, No. 4621. Category: Military. Value ✱✱.

Plate 44 – Official 'Britain Prepared' card issued by permission of H.M. Admiralty. Published exclusively by The Photochrom Co. Ltd, London. Categories: naval & shipping. Value ✱✱.

Plate 45 – One of the famous 'History & Traditions' series published by Gale & Polden. Category: military. Value ✱✱✱.

Plate 46 – The Volunteer Cyclist Corps published by Raphael Tuck & Sons, Oilette No. 9120. Category: military. Value ✱✱.

Plate 47 – Trooper 5th Lancers, review order, from the E.F.A. Military series. Category: military. Value ✱✱.

Plate 48 – An early World War I anti-German postcard drawn by E. Dupuis. One of the 'Leurs Caboches' series published in Paris. Category: military. Value ✱✱✱.

Plate 49 – Royal Artillery gun. Published by E.F.A. Military series. Category: military. Value ✱✱.

Plate 50 – Printed in Bavaria, a photographic card of the gunboat H.M.S. *Speedy*. Category: naval shipping. Value ✱✱.

Plate 51 – H.M.S. *Duncan* – from Tuck's 'Our Ironclad' series, No. 9183. Category: naval shipping. Value ✱✱✱.

Plate 52 – Romantic World War I theme, published by Reinthal & Newman. Category: W.W.I romantic. Value ✱✱.

Plate 53 – Saucy example of World War I glamour by an unsigned artist. Publisher and printer also unknown. Categories: comic and glamour. Value ✱.

Plate 54 – Russian sledging postcard painted by F. de Haenen from the series No. 31, 'Russia', published by A. & C. Black, London. Categories: semi-military and Russian topography. Value ✱✱✱.

Plate 55 – 'Fleur de Cerisier' by Alphonse Mucha. Early undivided back, published in France in 1898. Category: Art Nouveau. Value RRR.

Plate 56 – One of the colourful cards by Raphael Kirchner from the 'Mikado' series. Published and printed in Germany. Category: Art Nouveau. Value ****R.

Plate 57 – From the series 'Marionettes' by Raphael Kirchner with his ravishingly beautiful wife, Nina, pulling the strings. Category: Art Nouveau. Value ****R.

Plate 58 – An after-dinner rendezvous at the Great White City, London. A finely drawn card by an unsigned artist and published by Valentine's. Category: exhibitions. Value ***.

Plate 59 – One of Philip Boileau's bewitching ladies – who are almost always dressed for the Royal enclosure at Ascot! Published by Reinthal & Newman. Category: glamour. Value ***.

Plate 60 – 'Reflections' delicately portrayed by Harrison Fisher. Published by Reinthal & Newman. Category: glamour. Value ***.

Plate 61 – A postcard by an unsigned artist depicting the clean-cut charm of the typical American girl of the Edwardian period. Category: glamour. Value **.

Plate 62 – An amusing fantasy hat card drawn by Balho del Vella. Published in France. Categories: fantasy and glamour. Value ***.

Plate 63 – One of the desirable postcards by A. Penot from the series 'Sports d'hiver de la Parisienne'. Published and printed in France. Category: glamour. Value ****R.

Plate 64 – Another lovely girl drawn by Italian artist, S. Bompard. Published in Italy. Category: glamour. Value ***.

Plate 65 – Fabulous girl wearing an outrageously large hat drawn by Xavier Sager. Published and printed in France. Category, glamour. Value ***.

Plate 66 – 'Silhouettes Parisiennes, No. 4', another fantasy hat card – spiced with a glimpse of frilly undies and black stockings. Published and printed in France. Category, glamour. Value ***.

Plate 67 – Demure beauty by C. Barber. Published by the Carlton Publishing Co., London. Series No. 735. Category: glamour. Value **.

Plate 68 – Watercolour drawing by Clarence Underwood, published by Reinthal & Newman. Category: glamour. Value ***.

Plate 69 – From the Fidler-Lemunyan series, No. 5. Winsome American beauty drawn by Alice Luella Fidler in 1911. Category: glamour. Value **.

Plate 70 – More glamour by Harrison Fisher. Published by Reinthal & Newman. Category: glamour. Value ***.

Plate 71 – Unsigned glamour card published by the Inter-Art Co. from their 'Artistique' series. Category: glamour. Value **.

Plate 72 – One of the 'Furry Fashion' series published in 1910–1911. Categories: glamour and comic. Value **.

Plate 73 – Very fine lithographic poster-type advertisement for H. J. Heinz & Co. and their 57 Varieties. Early undivided back. Published and printed in the U.S.A. Category: advertising. Value RRR.

Plate 74 – Ocean Pier. Atlantic City, overprinted with advertising for Heinz. Published and printed in the U.S.A. Category: advertising. Value ****R.

Plate 75 – A very fine 'Grüss aus' poster-type advertisement for Shredded Wheat, 'mailed from the home of Shredded Wheat, Niagara Falls, N.Y.'. Category: advertising. Value RRR.

Plate 76 – The Marble Hall of the new premises of Debenham & Freebody from a painting by Byam Shaw. Published and printed in Great Britain. Category: advertising. Value ***.

Plate 77 – Poster-type advertisement for Fry's cocoa. Published and printed in Great Britain. Category: advertising. Value ****R.

Plate 78 – Macfarlane, Lang & Co.'s 'Sultana Sandwich', Series No. 1. Poster-type advertising card. Published by Macfarlane, Lang & Co. Category: advertising. Value ****R.

Plate 79 – Magnificent poster-type advertising postcard for Schweppes. Published and printed by Partridge & Love, Ltd, Bristol, England. Category: advertising. Value RRR.

Plate 80 – Gossages' pictorial series of poster-type advertisement for their carbolic soap. Category: advertising. Value ****R.

Plate 81 – Lightly embossed and gilded German greetings card. Published and printed in Germany. Category: special greetings ***.

Plate 82 – Theatre poster-type advertising for 'The Glad Eye' drawn by Bert Thomas. Published by the 'Echo' printing works, Loughborough, England. Category: theatre advertising. Value ✱✱✱.

Plate 83 – Gorgeous poster-type advertisement for J. M. Barrie's *Quality Street* drawn by Chris A. Suchel, with additional interest on reverse side which show overprinted details of a solitary performance scheduled at the Godalming Town Hall, 12 April 1904. Category: theatre advertising. Value ✱✱✱✱R.

Plate 84 – Poster advertisement for *The Four Just Men* by Edgar Wallace, drawn by Albert Morrow. Category: book advertising. Value RRR.

Plate 85 – One of the true postcard gems published by Raphael Tuck & Sons. Early undivided back, heavily embossed and gilded, 1902 coronation souvenir card, No. 611. Categories: Royalty and early Tuck's. Value RRR.

Plate 86 – Souvenir postcard commemorating the coronation of George V in 1911. Printed in Germany. Category: Royalty. Value ✱✱.

Plate 87 – Example of the work of E. Colombo. Published in Italy. Categories: glamour and horses. Value ✱✱✱.

Plate 88 – Early postcard published by Misch & Co., Series No. 838, 'With the Hounds', dated 1903. Category: Hunting. Value ✱✱✱.

Plates 89 and 90 – Two chromographed cards from Raphael Tuck & Sons 'Sporting' series, No. 1370. Categories: hunting and Tuck's. Value ✱✱.

Plate 91 – Typical seaside humour by Donald McGill. Category: comic. Value ✱✱.

Plate 92 – Early example of McGill humour, published by Joseph Asher, and printed in Holland. Category: comic. Value ✱✱✱.

Plate 93 – An amusing political card by Cynicus (Martin Anderson) published by The Cynicus Art Publishing Co., Leeds, England. Category: comic. Value ✱✱.

Plate 94 – A good 'Write-away' example from the Phil May

The leisured pace of
Philadelphia in 1906.

MARKET ST. WEST FROM 11th ST., PHILADELPHIA, PA.

'Cosmopolitan New York'.

3   Central Park, New York.
Raphael Tuck.

"Cosmopolitan New York."
Little Italy.—Vegetable Stands.

The Obelisk
Central Park

NEW YORK.

4 A city of
lights, Chicago by
night.

5 Lucerne,
Switzerland. A
room with a view
of the lake.

6 The City of
London. Hub of
the Empire.

Paris, Tour St. Jacques

From Maud Boeme –

7 Horse-drawn traffic in Paris.

DENVER, COLORADO.

7.12.04

U.S. MINT   STATE CAPITOL

Dear Ray. I was so pleased to receive your nice long letter the day I came home from Denver. I am glad you like the Cards. I think this is pretty, do you? I will send you a bunch Xmas from Auntie

ROCKY MT. SERIES NO. 14 PUB. BY CARSON HARPER CO. DENVER

8 An early American card with undivided back – from Denver.

9. NICE. La Jetée-Promenade et la Promenade des Anglais. ND. Phot.

9 When the English 'owned' the Riviera.

10 A German *Postkarte*. Issued by K. Hagen-Verlag of Offenburg.

11 A German holiday in Marienbad, now Marianske Lazne, Czechoslovakia.

12 The Berlin Opera; artist J. Miesler.

13 Early French street scene showing horse-drawn transport.

14 London's West End. The Hotel Cecil closed in 1930.

15 The Durley Dene at Bournemouth, the famous British south coast resort.

16 One of the elegant London rail hotels.

THE DINING ROOM, LIVERPOOL STREET HOTEL, LONDON, E.C.

17 Exeter's most exclusive hotel; West of England society meet for dinner.

DINING ROOM, ROUGEMONT HOTEL, EXETER

18 The Grosvenor Hotel adjoining Victoria Station; issued by Pitman's of London.

GROSVENOR · HOTEL · LONDON · S.W.

THE COSTUME SALON, HARRODS.

19 Harrods of London; famous the World over; a Raphael Tuck 'Oilette' card.

"CHURCHILL'S" BROADWAY AND FORTY-NINTH STREET, NEW YORK

20 'Churchill's' of New York, *c.* 1910; camera conscious diners in the foreground!

RESTAURANT "FRASCATI," LONDON.

21 Frascati's of London, survived many generations, but is now no more.

22 From the Raphael Tuck 'London Coliseum' series; tribute to a great London theatre.

23 Belle Vue, ballroom, Manchester, just before the First World War.

24 Where's that fire? Providence, Rhode Island, brigade.

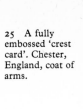

25 A fully embossed 'crest card'. Chester, England, coat of arms.

26 Another Raphael Tuck 'Oilette' card. 'Fighting the flames' by steam power, of course.

27 'Crest card'. Coat of arms of Paddington, London, England. Published by Ja-Ja.

Fighting the Flames.
THE BRIGADE AT WORK—CONNECTING THE HOSE.

28 The colours
on this card glow
when held to the
light. Samuel
Cupples of St.
Louis, U.S.A.

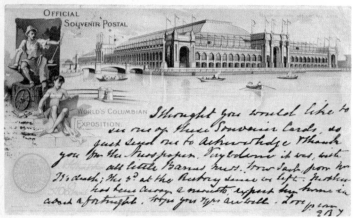

29 1893. Official
issue for the
World's
Columbian
Exposition.

30 Monte Carlo,
roulette table.
Issued by Giletta
frères, Nice.

722. — MONTE-CARLO. — Salle de Jeu. — Roulette.

31 An early embossed greetings card. Issued by L. Gross, Nice.

with very best wishes for the New Year –
J. V. W.
Hotel d'Angleterre Bordighera

Who is going to break the bank [at] Monte Carlo?

33 Pre-1905. The town hall at Basle, Switzerland.

Basel - Rathaus.

R. Glockner-Blattmann, Basel. 51.

35 German airship in combat with 'enemy aircraft'.

36 Changing guard at Buckingham Palace. Harry Payne.

37 A French
military airship
airborne above
Paris (1912).

38 Raphael
Tuck's 'Our
Fighting
Regiments'.
Dettingen, June
1743.

39 Raphael
Tuck's 'Military
in London' by
Harry Payne. A
new King's Guard
assembles at
Wellington
Barracks.

40 The Russo-Japanese War, 1904-5. The Russians in retreat by Caton Woodville.

41 The Greenjackets. A Gale & Polden card by Edgar A. Holloway.

42 Highland warriors on patrol. Another Raphael Tuck card by Harry Payne.

THE RIFLE BRIGADE.
The Colonel and Sergeant-Major.

ARGYLL & SUTHERLAND HIGHLANDERS

A Reconnoitering Patrol.

43 Royal Engineers on manoeuvres. Ettlinger's 'Life in our Army' series.

44 'Britain Prepared'.

45 Battle honours of a famous British regiment.

46 Summer militia camp. A Raphael Tuck 'Oilette' card.

47 Lancer in review order. E.F.A. Military Series.

48 German Death's Head Hussar. 'Several sorts of brute' according to the sender.

val Artillery Guns. Attention! 15 Field Gun
Detachment in Khaki.

49 Gun drill or.
the square. Field
artillery. E.F.A.
Military Series.

50 Royal Navy
gunboat
appropriately
named *Speedy*.
German card.

51 H.M.S.
Duncan, a British
Ironclad.

52 From the trenches with love, late 1914, issued by Reinthal and Newman.

"BEYOND CONTROL OF THE CENSOR"

53 Unsigned military 'glamour' card by an anonymous British publisher.

54 From 'Russia'. Painted by F. De Haenen and of British manufacture.

Sledging with the " Pristyashka " or Side-Horse.

55 'Fleur de Cerisier' – fine
example of art nouveau by
Alphonse Mucha.

Arrived home safe & sound   Love. Ruby

56 Raphael Kirchner art nouveau
card from the 'Mikado' series.

57 Raphael Kirchner art nouveau
card from the 'Marionettes' series.

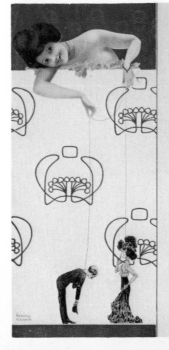

59 A glamorous
hat (Philip
Boileau). U.S.A.

58 Life-style of
Edwardian
gourmets.
Valentine's of
Great Britain.

60 'Reflections'
(Harrison Fisher).
U.S.A.

61 American
beauty. Artist
unknown.

63 Winter sports. A. Penot.

62 Fantasy hat card.
Source France.

65 *Dernière mode.*
By Xavier Sager.

Dernière Mode

64 A girl with a
dog. S. Bompard.

66 Fantasy hat
card. French card.

Silhouettes Parisiennes
Nº 4

La grande mode.
(Été)

THE RED HAT

67 A touch of British glamour. From Carlton of London.

PRETTY—COLD

Copyright. Edward Gross, N. Y.   AMERICAN GIRL NO. 17

69 American glamour girl. By Alice Luella Fidler.

68 Playing hard to get. By Clarence Underwood.

"... AND YET HER EYES CAN LOOK WISE"

70 Speculation. More American glamour by Harrison Fisher.

CECILIA

72 Furry fashio

THESE FEW "LINES" TO WISH YOU HAPPINESS, HEALTH, AND LUCK.

71 An English beauty issued by Inter-Art Co. of London.

73 Poster-type advertisement card. Printed for the Heinz company of Pittsburgh.

74 A later Heinz card. Ocean Pier, Atlantic City.

75 The Shredded Wheat Co., Niagara Falls, N.Y. Poster-type advertisement card.

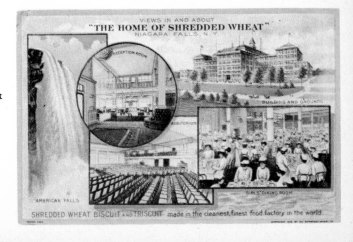

77 An English card, *c.* 1904, advertising Fry's Cocoa. Poster-type advertisement card.

DEBENHAM & FREEBODY'S NEW PREMISES.

THE MARBLE HALL.
From a painting by Byam Shaw

76 Advertising card from Debenham & Freebody.

78 A biscuit with the cup of cocoa? Macfarlane, Lang's to be sure! Poster-type advertisement card.

79 Schweppes
poster-type
advertisement
card printed in
Bristol, England.

In praise of carbolic soap.
ter-type advertisement card.

81 A German issue greetings card
with some embossing.

82 A poster-type
theatrical
advertisement
card. Strand
Theatre, London.

84 Edgar Wallace's most fam[e]
novel. (Artist Albert Morrow.)

83 Famous
play; famous
London theatre.

85 A Raphael Tuck embossed Edward VII coronation postcard.

86 George V and Queen Mary souvenir card. Printed in Saxony.

87 A sophisticated card and published in Italy.

88 'With the Hounds'. Designed in England and printed in Germany.

89 Raphael Tuck's 'Sporting' Series. Chromographed in Saxony.

90 From the same series.

British humour. Donald McGill's inimitable style.

Brighton.
Donald McGill.

93 British
political satire.

94 A 'write away' card from Raphael Tuck's 'Phil May' series.

95 Illustrated by Donald McGill. Publisher not known but printed in Bavaria.

DONT WASTE A SECOND, COME JUST AS YOU ARE

96 A 'write away' card. Published London; Artist Sydney Carter.

97 'Humour in Egypt – Cairo.' By L. Thackeray.

98 A Louis Wain card of character and charm.

99 Harvest supper. Printed in England. By Tom B.

101 Issued by F. Hartman, a German publisher, who introduced the 'divided back' card to Britain.

100 A Raphael Tuck embossed Christmas post card. Louis Wain style.

102 The Arcadians. Shaftesbury theatre, London. By Tom B.

103 An English seaside joke card originating from Germany.

104 'Agony Column'. Designed in England and printed in Prussia.

105 From the same series. Lucky fellow!

106 'I Dreamt I Dwelt in Marble Halls.'

107 A suffragette comic postcard. Printed in Holland.

108 'Dis am Susan' from the 'Little Darkies' series, published in England.

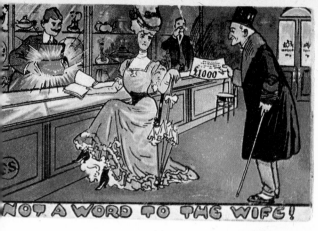

109 An English comic card. Signed F.S.

110 'Any Port in a Storm.' By Fleury.

111 What happened when the animals went to sea. Printed in Bavaria.

113 A Yorkshire saying.

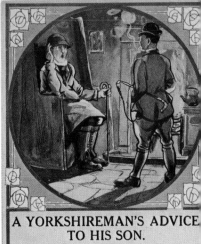

A YORKSHIREMAN'S ADVICE
TO HIS SON.

See All, Hear All, Say Nowt,
Eat All, Drink All, Pay Nowt,
And if ever tha does out for nowt
Allus do it for Thisen.

E. T. W. DENNIS & SONS, Ltd.   Scarborough & London.

"C. W. F. & Co." Series No. 237E.

Joe: "Your teeth are all Free Traders; I'll pull them out and
put you a set of my Protection grinders in."
Mr. Bull: "Not if I know it."

112 Joseph Chamberlain on tariff
reform.

114 Montage of
Edward VII
postage stamps.

115 Comic scene on the London underground.

116 Real pheasant feathers. Card manufactured in France.

117 Cut-out 'hold to light' card. D.R.G.M. of Germany.

119 Novelty
French card.
Mounted with
'ostrich feathers'.

MISS PAULINE CHASE

118 A novelty jewelled card.
Beagles of London.

120 A novelty strike
a match card.

IF FOR A SMOKE YOU
. ARE .
INCLINED

Just Strike a Match
on the Bear behind.

121 A Dutch coin card published in Germany by Max Heimbrecht.

10 Gulden	2½ Gulden	1 Gulden
18 Mark 87 Pfennig	4 M. 22 Pf.	1 M. 69 Pf.
19 Kronen 84 Heller	4 Kr. 96 H.	1 Kr. 98 H.
16 Shillings 6¼ Pence	4 sh. 1½ d.	1 sh. 7½ d.
20 Francs 85 Centimes	5 frs. 21 cts.	2 frs. 8 cts.
15 Kroner — Öre	3 Kr. 75 Ö.	1Kr. 50 Öre
7 Rubel / Roubles 81 Kop.	1 R. 95¼ Kp.	78 Kop.
4 Dollars ($) 2 Cents	1 $ ½ cts.	40 cts.

Wert in Gold. Valeur en or. Value in gold.

Niederlande. Netherlands.
Pays-Bas. Paises Bajos.
Nederland.

1 Gulden (Guilder, Florin, fl.) = 100 Cents.

122 Christmas fantasy greetings card. Printed in Bavaria.

123 Novelty courting card. Printed in Germany.

124 Midland Railway Comp[any]
advertising card.

125 C.P.R. Trans-Continental Express.

126 From Atlantic to Pacific.

127 GWR
engine: South
Wales coalfield.

8 A holiday in the Jura
ountains. Barreau of Paris.

129 Winter sports. J. Barreau of
Paris.

130 Third class dining car Great Northern Railway.

131 Drawing room car – Folkestone express. South Eastern & Chatham Railway.

132 The Great Central Railway. Anonymous British publisher.

133 Midland Railway Company advertising card.

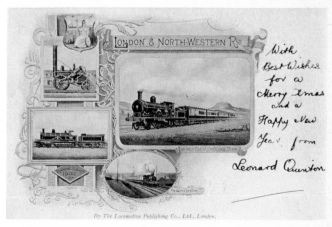

134 London & North-Western Railway card issued for the company's diamond jubilee in 1900.

135 The 'Southern Belle' in Victoria Station in the livery of the London, Brighton and South Coast Railway.

136 'Scotch Express'. North Eastern Railway; issued by *Locomotive Magazine*.

137 'Caledonian Express'; issued by Valentine of Dundee.

138 Great Northern Railway express taking on water. 'Reward' card. Raphael Tuck.

139 'Scotch' express arriving at London's King's Cross. Printed in Saxony.

140 London & North Western special. Liverpool – Euston liner express.

141 London Marylebone (Great Central Railway).

142 South-
ampton boat
train at Waterloo
(London & South
Western Railway).

143 Raphael
Tuck 'Oilette'.
Paddington:
Gateway to the
West of England.

144 Raphael
Tuck 'Oilette'.
'The Katy Flyer'.
Missouri, Kansas
and Texas
Railway.

145 Pennsylvania Railway. Coal train (sixty cars) hauled by three engines.

146 The Rigi Rack Railway in Switzerland.

147 Manchester–Nashua Electric Railway, New Hampshire, c. 1910.

MANCHESTER-NASHUA ELECTRIC RAILWAY.

S.S. "PERSIA."
7,951 Tons.   11,000 h.p.

P AND O

148   Port side
out starboard
side home.
P and O shipping lin

*Port Said. 1907. My Dear Elsie. We have
had a rough trip from Marseilles. Eva is very well
[illegible] trust love to all. Kind [illegible] to Mr [illegible] Mary [illegible]*

LENGTH 790 FT.   BREADTH 88 FT.   DEPTH (MOULDED) 60 FT.   TONNAGE 33,000.   HORSE POWER 70,000   SPEED 25 KNOTS.
R.M.S. "MAURETANIA" (CUNARD LINE.)

149   The
launching of the
R.M.S.
Mauretania in
1906. Designed
in bas-relief.

White Star Liner "Titanic"

150   1912. The
ill-fated White
Star Liner
Titanic.

151 Mississippi roll along . . . . until the end of time. Milwaukee publisher.

STEAMBOAT "CITY OF ST. LOUIS."

Oct 6 1905
Leave here tonight
for San Francisco, due there on the
10th – love R.L.T

COMPAGNIE DE NAVIGATION MIXTE MARSEILLE
Paquebots - Poste Francais

BÔNE (ALGÉRIE)

Départ de MARSEILLE pour PHILIPPEVILLE et BÔNE
Le Jeudi à Midi.
Départ de BÔNE et PHILIPPEVILLE pour MARSEILLE
Le Dimanche à Midi de PHILIPPEVILLE.

152 French steam packet in service between Marseille and Bône in North Africa.

153 Ship's drawing room scene. Cunard line, *Campania* and *Lucania*.

Drawing Room: CUNARD R.M.S. "CAMPANIA" "LUCANIA"

154 Social Hall of The Royal Mail Steam Packet Company's *Amazon* cruise ship.

155 The Smoking Room of the same ship.

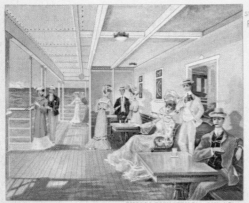

156 Outside the Smoking Room of the *Amazon* we find a verandah.

I — 8 HP. single cylinder
de Dion-Bouton Tonneau
PUTEAUX

Puteaux (Seine)

157 The De Dion Bouton was the first truly practical small car.

THE QUEENS CHOICE.

158 The Wolseley-Siddeley made in Great Britain between 1905-9.

159 Lancashire by the sea. Published by Wm Berry of Bradford.

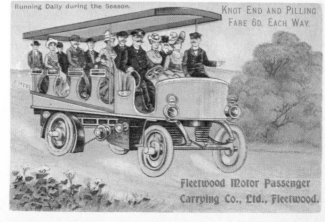

Running Daily during the Season.

KNOT END AND PILLING
FARE 6D. EACH WAY.

Fleetwood Motor Passenger
Carrying Co., Ltd., Fleetwood.

160 This view of Deansgate, Manchester, England, was printed in Bavaria.

161 Typical north European street scene. Christiana, Norway.

162 Raphael Tuck 'Oilette' card. Alexandria-Cairo express. Egyptian State railways.

163 Steam power in agriculture. Ruddocks, printers, Lincoln, England.

4 More steam power from the ne manufacturer.

165 Chromotype English card. Postmarked 1904.

Improved Single Cylinder Portable Steam Engine
MADE BY
CLAYTON & SHUTTLEWORTH, Ltd., LINCOLN.

166   Market Street, San Francis
before and after the earthquake.

167   Train accident somewhere in England.

168   London policeman. Symbol of
law and order.

ACCIDENT ON ZIG ZAG, APRIL 1901.   PHOTO. BY LITHGOW STUDIOS.

169 Chinese court in session. A bizarre card from Hong Kong.

170 The Crooked House, Himley, presented remarkable optical illusions. Bizarre English card.

171 Wm McKinley, twenty-fourth president of the U.S.A., was shot by an anarchist and died on 6 September 1901.

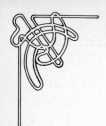

173 Christmas greetings.

174 Christmas greetings.

175 Insert card from the English magazine *Weekly Tale-Teller*.

176 An American embossed Christmas card.

177 An embossed English Christmas card printed in Germany.

178 Father
Christmas card.
Published in
London but
printed in Berlin.

179 A Raphael
Tuck Christmas
card designed in
bas-relief.

180 An early
American
Valentine card.

 A German birthday greetings
d.

182 Easter greetings.
Embossed and inlaid. Ettlinger
of London and New York.

183 Another
early American
Valentine card.

184 An
American
Thanksgiving
greetings card.

185 The hands
of the clock can be
turned to the
appointed hour.
Chromographed
in Berlin.

186 A 'hands
across the sea'
greetings card.
Printed in
England.

187 A children's card. Illustrated in England by Ethel Parkinson.

THE PROOF OF THE PUDDING LIES IN THE EATING

188 A German children's card.

GOLLIWOGG RESCUED

This is a very pretty P.C. isn't it. I think it ought to be one of Baby's hossy. Don't you yours by T.

189 Raphael Tuck 'Golliwogg' art series. Illustrated by Florence Upton.

190 From a Lincoln birthday centennial series published in the U.S.A. in 1909.

191 Illustrated by Klein. Published by 'Alpha' of London.

192 Jewish New Year card. Published by Williamsburg of New York, but made in Germany.

Printed in Great Britain by Jarrold and Sons Ltd, Norwich

series No. 1294, published by Raphael Tuck & Sons. Category: comic. Value ****R.

Plate 95 – Another design from the drawing board of Blackheath artist, Donald McGill. Category: comic. Value **.

Plate 96 – 'Write-away' drawn by Sydney Carter and published by Hildesheimer & Co. Category: comic. Value **.

Plate 97 – Middle Eastern humour by Lance Thackeray. Published by Tuck's from series 'Humour in Egypt – Cairo', No. 9547. Category: comic. Value ***.

Plate 98 – One of the very fine postcards by Louis Wain with advertising overprinted for Jacksons hats and boots. Category: comic and advertising. Value ****R.

Plate 99 – One of Nottingham born artist Tom Browne's comic series. Published by Davidson Bros, No. 2601 *Country Life*. Category: comic. Value ***.

Plate 100 – Embossed chromograph published by Tuck's, 'Christmas' series, No. 8142. Category: embossed greetings. Value ***.

Plate 101 – Early bathing beauties, published by F. Hartmann. Categories: glamour and bathing beauties. Value ***.

Plate 102 – Theatre advertising for 'The Arcadians', published by Miles of Wardour Street, London. Category: theatre advertising. Value ***.

Plate 103 – Saucy seaside comic initialled E.W. Category: comic. Value *.

Plates 104 and 105 – Two examples of Misch & Stock's 'Agony Column' series. Misch & Co., also produced a similar series entitled 'Addled Ad's'. Category: comic. Value ***.

Plate 106 – One of the vignette type comics published by W. Mackenzie & Co. Category: comic. Value **.

Plate 107 – A comic 'Suffragette' Valentine postcard. Categories: comic, Valentine, and political. Value ****R.

Plate 108 – From the 'Little Darkies' series, No. 521, published by A. M. Davis & Co. Categories: children and comic. Value **.

Plate 109 – Wry humour by F.S. Category: comic. Value *.

Plate 110 – A Star series comic card drawn by H. Fleury. Category: comic. Value **.

Plate 111 – Delightful comic animal postcard published by Ernest Mister, Series 179. Category: comic. Value **.

Plate 112 – Political humour drawn by Arthur Moreland and published by C. W. Faulkner, Series No. 248F. Categories: comic and political. Value ***.

Plate 113 – One of the Yorkshire Arms, Toasts, and Sayings series, No. 56, published by E. T. W. Dennis & Sons Ltd, Scarborough. Categories: comic and verse. Value ***.

Plate 114 – A hand done stamp montage card – a pastime much favoured in Edwardian times. Category: novelty. Value ***.

Plate 115 – London-Tube comic scene by George Davey. Category: comic. Value ***.

Plate 116 – Novelty card showing a beautiful pheasant with real feathers. Published and printed in France. Category: novelty. Value ****R.

Plate 117 – Coloured cut-out hold-to-light card produced in Germany. When H.T.L. the message, windows and moon light up. Category: novelty. Value ***.

Plate 118 – Bejewelled and tinted photograph of Pauline Chase. Published by J. Beagles, London. Categories: theatrical and novelty. Value ***.

Plate 119 – Tinted photographic card of a beauty wearing a real ostrich feathered hat. Published and printed in France. Category: novelty glamour. Value ****R.

Plate 120 – Teddy Bear card with sandpaper attached to his seat for match-striking. Published by H.B., London. Category: novelty. Value ***.

Plate 121 – One of the very desirable embossed, silvered and gilded Coin cards, showing Dutch coinage. Published and printed in Germany by Max Heimbrecht. Category: coinage. Value ****R.

Plate 122 – Christmas angels, published by Ernest Nister. Category: greetings. Value **.

Plate 123 – Romance between a Teddy Bear and a Matchstick

girl. Published by B.B. (Birn Bros). Categories: children and comic. Value ✳✳✳.

Plate 124 – Fine advertisement card published by the Midland Railway Company. Category: railway advertising. Value ✳✳✳.

Plate 125 – Railway poster-type advertisement for the Canadian Pacific Railway. Category: railway poster-advertising. Value RRR.

Plate 126 – A different version of poster-advertising for the Canadian Pacific Railway. Category: railway advertising. Value RRR.

Plate 127 – Great Western Railway coal train leaving for the docks drawn by H. Fleury, and published for the Star series. Category: railway. Value ✳✳✳.

Plate 128 – Magnificent railway poster-advertisement showing picturesque Jura via the Paris–Lyon–Méditerranée Railway. Category: railway advertising. Value RRR.

Plate 129 – 'Sports d'hiver Chamonix' via the Paris-Lyons & à la Méditerranée Railway. Category: railway advertising. Value RRR.

Plate 130 – Interior view of a third-class dining car, Great Northern Line. Category: railway. Value ✳✳✳.

Plate 131 – South Eastern & Chatham Railway, Official postcard published by McCorquodale & Co. Ltd showing the drawing-room car, Folkestone Express. Category: railway. Value ✳✳✳.

Plate 132 – Fabulous vignette, undivided back, poster-type advertisement for the Great Central Railway. Category: railway advertising. Value RRR.

Plate 133 – Railway Official card advertising the Midland Route. Category: railway. Value ✳✳✳.

Plate 134 – Another superb poster-type advertisement for the London & North Western Railway. Published by the Locomotive Publishing Co., London. Category: railway advertising. Value RRR.

Plate 135 – 'The Southern Belle' – fine close-up at Victoria Station. Published by the Locomotive Publishing Co., London. Category: railway. Value ✳✳✳.

179

Plate 136 – The 'Scotch Express' postcard issued by the Locomotive Magazine series. Category: railway. Value ***.

Plate 137 – Close-up of the Caledonian Express. Published by Valentine's & Son. Category: railway. Value ***.

Plate 138 – A London County Council Reward card published by Raphael Tuck & Sons. Categories: railway and reward cards. Value **.

Plate 139 – Arrival of the 'Scotch Express' at King's Cross Station. Published by Misch & Co., No. 331, 'Noted Trains' series. Category: railway. Value ***.

Plate 140 – Another from the 'Noted Trains' series, the special Liner express arriving at Euston Station. Category: railway. Value ***.

Plate 141 – Southport train at Marylebone Station, 'Noted Trains' series. Category: railway. Value ***.

Plate 142 – The Southampton boat train at Waterloo, 'Noted Trains' series, drawn by H. Fleury. Category: railway. Value ***.

Plate 143 – Paddington Station, G.W.R. interior, published by Tuck's Oilette series, No. 9279, 'London Railway Stations'. Category: railway. Value ***.

Plate 144 – The 'Katy Flyer' published by Tuck's 'Railways of the World' series, Oilette No. 9274. Category: railways. Value ***.

Plate 145 – Pennsylvania Railway coal train of sixty cars. Published by the Locomotive Publishing Co. Category: railway. Value ***.

Plate 146 – The Rigi Rack Railway, Switzerland, published by Tuck's, 'Railways of the World' series, No. 9274. Category: railway. Value ***.

Plate 147 – Manchester-Nashua Electric Railway. Published by John B. Varick Co., Manchester, N.H., U.S.A. Category: railway. Value **.

Plate 148 – Ship advertising card for the P. & O. Line. S.S. *Persia* with paquebot mark on reverse. Categories: shipping and advertising. Value ***.

Plate 149 – Bas-relief card of R.M.S. *Mauretania* (Cunard Line).

Alliance series, No. 125, patented by Taber Bas-Relief Co. Categories: shipping and novelty. Value ∗∗.

Plate 150 – White Star Liner, R.M.S. *Titanic*. Published by Millar & Lang in their National series. Category: shipping. Value ∗∗∗.

Plate 151 – The 'City of St. Louis' steamboat leaving for San Francisco. Category: American shipping. Value ∗∗∗.

Plate 152 – Early undivided back shipping advertising for the Marseille Navigation Company. Category: French shipping. Value ∗∗∗∗R.

Plate 153 – Standard view of the drawing-rooms aboard Cunard liners. Category: shipping. Value ∗∗.

Plates 154, 155 & 156 – Three beautiful interior views of the R.M.S.P. *Amazon*. Category: shipping interiors. Value ∗∗∗.

Plate 157 – Advertising card issued by De Dion-Bouton Co. Ltd showing an artist drawn close-up of the 8 HP. single cylinder de Dion-Bouton Tonneau. Category: transport. Value ∗∗∗.

Plate 158 – 'The Queen's Choice' advertising card for the Wolseley Tool & Motor Car Co. Ltd – postmarked 1908. Category: transport and advertising. Value ∗∗∗∗R.

Plate 159 – Comic type of advertising card for the Fleetwood Motor Passenger Carrying Co. Ltd., Fleetwood. Category: transport and advertising. Value ∗∗∗.

Plate 160 – A traffic-jam of trams in Deansgate, Manchester. Category: transport. Value ∗∗.

Plate 161 – Close-up of Norwegian transport. Category: transport. Value ∗∗∗.

Plate 162 – The Alexandria–Cairo Express from Tuck's 'Wide Wide World' series, No. 9329, 'Famous Expresses'. Category: railway. Value ∗∗∗.

Plate 163 – Superb close-up of Clayton & Shuttleworth Ltd, Lincoln, agricultural traction engine, printed by Ruddock's of Lincoln. Category: transport and machinery. Value ∗∗∗∗R.

Plate 164 – The improved single-cylinder portable steam engine close-up, also made by the above company, and printed by Ruddock's. Category: transport and machinery. Value ∗∗∗∗R.

Plate 165 – Poster-advertisement for Premier Bicycles, published by David Allen in 1904. Category: poster advertising and transport. Value RRR.

Plate 166 – Before and after the earthquake, Market Street, San Francisco. Category: disasters. Value **.

Plate 167 – Railway accident. Category: disasters. Value ***.

Plate 168 – Tuck's Oilette No. 9015, 'London Life' series. Category: Tuck's artistic. Value **.

Plate 169 – A Chinese Court, published in Hong-Kong by K.M. & Co. Category: Chinese interest. Value ***.

Plate 170 – View of the bar room at the Crooked House Inn at Himley in Staffordshire. Category: topographical inns and public houses. Value *.

Plate 171 – The National McKinley Memorial with inset portraits of President and Mrs McKinley. Published by Hugh C. Leighton & Co., Portland, U.S.A. Category: American political and topographical. Value ***.

Plate 172 – The Language of Keys – glows when held-to-light, published by Alfred Stiebel. Category: language greetings card. Value ****R.

Plate 173 – Early Tuck's Christmas series, No. 1744, with undivided back. Category: Father Christmas greetings. Value ***.

Plate 174 – Tuck's Oilette Christmas Greetings card, No. 8320. Category: Christmas greetings. Value ***.

Plate 175 – Hay-raking rural scene, one of the insert cards given away with the *Weekly Tale-Teller* magazine. Category: rural. Value *.

Plate 176 – Embossed and gilded Christmas bells. Category: Christmas greetings. Value ***.

Plate 177 – Embossed Christmas greetings card published by the Woolstone Bros of London. Category: Christmas greetings. Value ***.

Plate 178 – Gilded Christmas greetings published by E. A. Schwerdtfeger & Co., London. Category: Christmas greetings. Value ***.

Plate 179– Raphael Tuck & Sons 'Merry Christmas' card in the 'New Year' series, No. 8376. Category: greetings. Value ∗∗∗.

Plate 180– An American Valentine card on a silvered background. Category: Valentine greetings. Value ∗∗∗∗R.

Plate 181– Lightly embossed and gilded German greetings card. Category: greetings. Value ∗∗.

Plate 182– Beautifully embossed and gilded Easter greetings published by Max Ettlinger. Category: Easter greetings. Value ∗∗∗.

Plate 183– Another attractive American Valentine greetings card. Category: Valentine greetings. Value ∗∗∗∗R.

Plate 184– An American postcard for Thanksgiving day. Category: greetings. Value ∗∗.

Plate 185– One of the very fine Tuck's mechanical postcards – the hands of the clock can be turned. Category: novelty. Value ∗∗∗∗R.

Plate 186– A typical version of the popular 'Hands Across the Sea' greetings. Category: shipping and greetings. Value ∗∗.

Plate 187– A Dutch children's scene by Ethel Parkinson, published by C. W. Faulkner. Category: children. Value ∗∗∗.

Plate 188– Another postcard published by C. W. Faulkner of Dutch children, drawn this time by I.M.J. Category: children. Value ∗∗.

Plate 189– 'Golliwog rescued' from one of the Florence Upton Golliwog series, published by Tuck. Categories: children and comic. Value ∗∗∗∗R.

Plate 190– The Abraham Lincoln Centennial Souvenir card from Lincoln's Birthday series, No. 1. Category: American commemorative. Value ∗∗∗∗R.

Plate 191– A bunch of grapes painted by C. Klein. Category: fruit & flowers. Value ∗∗.

Plate 192– A Jewish New Year postcard, published by Williamsburg Art Co., New York. Category: Jewish greetings. Value ∗∗∗∗R.

6 *A Quick Reference Guide to Postcards*

The prices of early postcards fluctuate from country to country and from dealer to dealer. They also have a habit of changing almost overnight; what is fashionable today could be as dead as cold mutton tomorrow, so any attempt to put fixed price-tags on postcards is impossible. We have, therefore, continued to use our 'rarity factor' system in the compilation of the following lists of categories and artists. We hope that they will show that the hobby of collecting picture postcards caters for every taste and every pocket. There are fine prospects for investment in a collection of postcards, but this is not the prime factor; collections are meant to be enjoyed, the hunt to increase them intended to be fun, and the choice of themes a matter of individual taste.

POSTCARD CATEGORIES AND THEIR RARITY FACTORS

Advertising

Celebrated Poster series published by Raphael Tuck & Sons Ltd	****R
Other good poster-types, e.g. Fry's, Suchar's Quaker Oats, Lemco, etc.	****R
Goss Pottery cards, published by W. H. Goss	****R
Trent Pottery cards, published by Trent Bridge Publishing Co.	***

Non-poster advertising cards, i.e. projecting particular
firms or wares   **

Advertising 'give-away's' (insert cards), e.g. Shurey's,
Christian Novels, Weldons' Bazaar, The Field, Tiny
Totts, T.A.T. etc.   from * to ***

Reward cards, e.g. Cadbury's, County Councils, School
Boards etc.   **

Animals

Photographic animal studies by known photographers   **

All other photographic types of postcard showing birds,
zoos, wild animals, etc.   *

Artist-signed animal sketches by Louis Wain   ****R

Artist-signed sketches by Arthur Thiele, Cecil Aldin, etc.   ***

Artist-signed sketches by Eugene Valter, 'Mac', Florence
Valter, etc.   **

Art Reproduction

Top quality postcards by Misch & Co., Stengel & Co.,
C. W. Faulkner, etc.   **

Early series published by Raphael Tuck & Sons Ltd.   ***

'Star' series and similar types   *

Art Nouveau – unsigned early postcards   ****R

Artists – See special section

Aviation

All early cards with 'flown' cachets   RRR

Early aeroplanes – close-ups   ****R

Early aeroplanes with photographic insets of pilots   ***

Aviation meetings   RRR

Early dirigibles and airships – close-ups   ****R

Early balloons – close-ups   ****R

World War I Zeppelins – close-ups   ****R

World War I aircraft – close-ups   ***

World War II aircraft – close-ups   ***

Modern Commercial Air Lines – close-ups of aircraft   *

Gale & Polden – R.F.C. postcards   ***
Aircraft series published by Raphael Tuck & Sons Ltd   ***

Bathing
Early bathing beauties (embossed)   ***
Comic bathing beauties (embossed)   ***
Early bathing scenes and beauties (coloured, silvered, etc.)   **

Buildings
Edifices from abbeys to village crosses   *

Children
Unsigned sketches of nursery rhyme themes, child
    studies, babies, fairy stories, etc.   **

Cinematic
Pre-1930 film stars – photographic studies   ***
Post-1930 film stars – photographic studies   **
Early photographic views of cinemas   ***
Early sketches of Felix, Mickey Mouse, and other Disney
    characters   ***

Coaching
Early close-up of horse-drawn coaching cards   **
Coaching series by Maggs   **

Coins and Paper Money
Embossed coins of all countries   ****R
Printed series showing coins   ***
Postcards showing banknotes   ***

Comic
Unsigned artist-drawn humour covering all aspects of
    social comment   **
Unsigned artist-drawn 'Write-away' types of the pre-
    1910 period   ***

186

Costume
National dress and photographic cards recording fashion
    to World War II   *

Disasters
Photographic cards depicting earthquakes, fires, floods,
    landslips, storm damage, and volcanic eruptions   **
Railway smashes, aeroplane and motor crashes   ****R
Tram accidents   ****R

Exhibitions
Postcards featuring exhibition views with appropriate
    postmarks   ****R
Postcards featuring pre-1900 exhibition views which are
    not postally used   **
Postcards featuring Edwardian exhibition views which
    are not postally used   *

Fantasy
Fantasy heads – e.g. black and white sketches of heads of
    state composed of nudes   ****R
Fantasy babies – e.g. babies profusely shown in odd situa-
    tions   **
Hidden faces in mountains, etc., mainly published in Ger-
    many   ***

Fire Stations, Firemen, and Engines
Early horse-drawn fire engines – close-ups   ****R
Motorized fire engines – close-ups   ****R
Firemen in action – putting out fires etc.   ***
Fire stations   **

Folklore
Village history and traditions   **

Greetings

Early German gilded and/or embossed	***
Pre-1900 Grüss Aus type postcards	***
Jewish New Year cards	****R
Valentine postcards	***
Christmas, Easter, Thanksgiving, Hallowe'en, St Patrick's Day, etc.	**
Glossy greetings with or without deckled edges	*

Heraldic

City crests published by Ja-Ja	***
Heraldic embossed series published by Raphael Tuck & Sons Ltd	****R
Crested view cards	**

Industrial

Mining, engineering, men at work in heavy industry	***

Language cards

E.g. flowers, fruit, stamps, keys, vegetables, etc.	**

Large letter and date cards – pre-1910

	**

Maps

Geographical series	*

Military

Boer War anti-British cartoons	****R
Boer War photographic scenes	****R
Boer War artist-signed sketches	****R
Boxer Rebellion – cartoon types	RRR
Russo-Japanese War – anti-Russian cartoons	****R
Military sketches of battle scenes and uniforms etc., artist-signed	***
Daily Mail, illustrated newspapers, etc., battle scenes	**
Family photograph types illustrating soldiers in uniform	**

| Military camps, barracks, etc. | ** |
| Military camps with appropriate camp postmarks | *** |

Motoring

Close-ups of early motor cars and motoring	***
Close-ups of motor-cycles with or without side-cars	****R
Close-ups of charabancs	**
Close-ups of motor-buses	***
Brooklands – motor-racing	RRR

Music, Composers, etc.

| Musical scores and photographs of composers | ** |

Novelty

Aluminium	***
Celluloid – in undamaged condition	***
Composite sets, e.g. sets of cards which are assembled to form the faces of Napoleon, the Kaiser, etc.	RRR
Model cut-outs – houses, dolls, dolls clothing, etc.	****R
Leather	***
Perfume sachets	***
Peat postcards	***
Wood postcards	***
Gramophone record cards	****R
Jig-saw and zag-zaw puzzle cards	RRR
Hold-to-light – transparencies – Meteor type	RRR
Hold-to-light – black and white – chameleon colour change type	****R
Hold-to-light – puzzle cards, e.g. 'Find the submarine, Zeppelin, etc.'	****R
Hold-to-light – cut-out variety	***
Squeakers	***
Panel, bookmark, giant and midget cards	**

Patriotic

| Flags, patriotic verses and songs, etc. | ** |

Political

Artist-signed cartoons of early politicians	***
Photographic postcards showing political figures, election announcements	**

Religion

Sets of the Ten Commandments	****R
Sets of the Lord's Prayer	***
Sets of Stations of the Cross	****R
Faith, Hope and Charity cards	**
S.P.G. and other Missionary cards	*

Romance

Edwardian romantic themes – usually issued in sets of six	**
Proverbs with romantic themes	**

Royalty

Early cards showing Queen Victoria and her family	****R
Edwardian Royal family photographs	**
Royal processions – Coronation, Funeral, etc.	*
Royal visits and special occasions	***
Royalty postcards other than British	***

Rural

Farming, traditional industry, pastoral scenes, etc.	*

Theatrical

David Allen poster-type advertisements for theatrical productions	***
Similar miscellaneous types of poster cards	**
Photographic Play Pictorials – showing scenes from plays, etc.	**
Pierrots, concert parties, etc.	*
Autographed photographs of Edwardian actors and actresses	***
Photographs of Edwardian actors and actresses	**

Transport

Close-ups of locomotives	***
Railway official card issued by railway company	**
Close-ups of traction engines	****R
Poster-type advertising for railway company	RRR
Tramway commemorative cards – openings, etc.	****R
Tramway 'In Memoriam' cards	****R
Tram accidents	****R
Close-ups of trams	***
Decorated ceremonial trams	***
Good street scenes with reasonably close-views of trams	**
Pamlin reproductions of trams	*
Close-ups of merchant ships	**
Close-ups of naval vessels	**
Shipping disasters, e.g. the sinking of the *Titanic*	****R
Ship wrecks	***

Watermills and Windmills

Good close-up views	**

Woven Silk cards

By Thomas Stevens and W. Grant	****R

Named Artists and Their Rarity Factors

Name	Subject	Rarity Factor
Abeille Jack	Glamour	****R
Aldin Cecil	Advertising, animals, etc.	***
Asti Angelo	Beautiful women	**
Attwell Mabel Lucie	Children	*
Bairnsfather Bruce	World War I Humour	**
Ball Wilfred	Scenic	*
Bamber George A.	Comic	**
Barham S.	Children	***
Barber C. W.	Glamour	**

191

Name	Subject	Rarity Factor
Barnes G.	Comic	**
Barribal	Glamour and Children	**
Becker C.	Military	****R
Belcher George	Comic	****R
Berthon Paul	Art Nouveau	RRR
Bertiglia	Glamour and Children	***
Bianchi	Glamour	***
Bianco T.	Political cartoons	****R
Biggar J. L.	Comic	**
Billings M.	Flowers and Fruit	**
Boileau Philip	Glamour	***
Bompard S.	Glamour	***
Borrow W. H.	Scenic (water-colour)	**
Bradley William H.	Art Nouveau	RRR
Bradshaw P. V.	Comic	****R
Breanski de A.	Scenic	**
Browne Tom	Comic	***
	Advertisement types	****R
	Dutch scenes	***
Brundage Frances	Children	***
Brunelleschi	Art Nouveau	RRR
Buchanan Fred	Comic	***
Bull Rene	Comic	***
Burton F. W.	Scenic	*
Busi A.	Glamour	***
Butcher Arthur	Glamour and Comic	**
Buxton Dudley	Comic	**
Caldecott Randolph	Children	**
Carrere F. Ouillon	Glamour	****R
Carruthers W.	Scenic	*
Carter Reg.	Comic	**
Carter Sydney	Comic	**
Cassiers Henri	Advertisement, Exhibitions	***
Christie G.	Comic	**
Clapsaddle Ellen	Children	***
Cobbe B.	Animals	**

Name	Subject	Rarity Factor
Colombo	Glamour and Children	***
Comicus	Comic	**
Copping Harold	Religious and Caricature	**
Corbella Tom	Glamour	***
Corke C. Essenhigh	Scenic	*
Cowham H.	Advertisement and Comic	***
Crackerjack	Comic	**
Crombie C. M.	Comic	***
Cubley Hadfield	Scenic	*
Cynicus	Comic and Novelty	**
Daniell Eva	Art Nouveau	RRR
Dauber	Comic	**
Davey George	Comic	**
Dinah	World War II Humour	***
Drummond Norah	Animals	**
Dupuis Émile	Caricaturist	***
Dwig	Comic	***
Earnshaw H.	Comic	**
Ebner Pauli	Children	**
Ellam	Comic	***
Endacott S.	Scenic	**
Fabiano F.	Glamour	***
Feure Georges de	Art Nouveau	RRR
Fidler Alice	Beauty	**
Fisher Harrison	Beauty	**
Fleury H.	Comic	**
Flower Charles	Scenic	**
Folkard Charles	Children	***
Fontan Leo	Glamour	****R
French Annie	Art Nouveau	RRR
Fuller Edmund G.	Comic	***
Furniss Harry	Political cartoons	***

Name	Subject	Rarity Factor
Gallon R.	Scenic	*
Gassaway	Children	***
Gibson C. Dana	Fantasy Glamour	**
Gilson T.	Comic	**
Govey Lilian	Children	***
Grasset Eugene	Art Nouveau	RRR
Grimes	World War II Humour	****R
Guillaume A.	Comic and erotica	***
Hager Nini	Art Nouveau	****R
Hannaford	Scenic	*
Harbour Jennie	Fashion and Glamour	****R
Hardy Dudley	Comic	***
Hardy Florence	Children	**
Hassall John	Comic and Advertising	***
Hayes F. W.	Scenic	*
Hayes Sydney	Animals	**
Herouard	Glamour	****R
Hier Professor van	Scenic	**
Hilton Alf	Comic	**
Holloway E. A.	Military	***
Hyde Graham	Comic	***
Ibbetson Ernest	Comic and Military	***
Jarach A.	Glamour	****R
Jotter	Scenic	**
Jozsa Carl	Art Nouveau	RRR
I.M.J.	Children	**
Kennedy A.	Animals	**
King Jessie Marian	Art Nouveau	RRR
Kinsella E. P.	Comic	**
Kirchner Raphael	Art Nouveau	****R
Klein C.	Flowers and Fruit	***
Koehler M.	Art Deco	****R
Kyd	Comic and Caricature	***

194

Name	Subject	Rarity Factor
Lambert H. Marsh	Children	***
Leonnec G.	Glamour	***
Lessieux E.	Art Nouveau	RRR
	Scenic	**
Lewin F. G.	Comic	**
Longstaffe E.	Scenic	*
Ludgate	Comic	**
Ludovici A.	Comic and Caricature	***
'Mac'	Animals	**
McGill Donald	Comic	**
McNeill J.	Military	***
Mackain F.	Comic	***
Maggs J. C.	Coaching	**
Mailick	Greetings/Embossed art	***
Mair Henrietta Willebeek le	Children	****R
Manavian V.	Comic	***
Mastroianni	Fantasy Art	**
Matthison W.	Scenic	*
Maurice Reg.	Comic	**
Mauzan	Glamour	***
May Phil	Comic	****R
Menpes Mortimer	Scenic	**
Mercer Joyce	Art Deco	****R
Meunier Henri	Art Nouveau	RRR
Meunier Suzanne	Glamour	****R
Millière Maurice	Glamour	****R
Monestier C.	Glamour	**
Monier Maggy	Glamour	****R
Moreland Arthur	Comic	***
Morris M.	Scenic	**
Mouton G.	Art Nouveau	****R
M.S.M.	Beauty	***
Mucha Alphonse	Art Nouveau	****R
Nanni	Glamour	***
Nash A. A.	Children	**

		Rarity
Name	Subject	Factor
Newton G. E.	Scenic	*
Noble Ernest	Comic	**
Norman Parsons	Scenic	*
Nystrom Jennie	Nordic Art	****R
O'Beirne F.	Military	****R
O'Neill Rose	Kewpies (children)	****R
Orens	Caricatures	****R
Outhwaite I.	Children	***
Owen Will	Comic	****R
Palmer Sutton	Scenic	*
Parkinson Ethel	Children	***
Parlett Harry	Comic	**
Payne Arthur	Scenic	**
Payne Harry	Military and Rural	***
Pearse Susan	Children	**
Peltier L.	Glamour	***
Penot A.	Glamour	****R
Pepin Maurice	Glamour	***
Pfaff	Scenic	**
Phillimore R. P.	Scenic	**
Pirkis	Comic	**
Pressland A.	Scenic	*
Pyp	Comic	**
Quatremain W.	Scenic	*
Quinton A. R.	Scenic	**
Rappini	Glamour	***
Richardson Agnes	Children	**
Roberts Violet	Comic	***
Robinson-Heath	Comic	****R
Rostro	Caricaturist	****R
Rountree Harry	Comic	***

Name	Subject	Rarity Factor
Sager Xavier	Clamour and Political cartoons	****R
Sepheard G.	Comic	**
Shand C. E.	Children	***
Simonetti	Glamour	**
Smith J. Wilcox	Children	**
Sowerby Millicent	Children	***
Spatz	Comic	**
Spurgin Fred	Comic	**
Studdy George	Comic	**
Tam Jean	Glamour	***
Tarrant Margaret	Children	**
Tempest D.	Comic	**
Tempest Margaret	Children	**
Terzi	Glamour	***
Thackeray Lance	Comic	***
Thiele Arthur	Comic	***
Thomas Bert	Comic	***
Twelvetrees H.	Children	**
Upton Florence	Golliwogs (children)	****R
Usaba L.	Glamour	**
Valter Eugene	Animals	*
Vallotton Felix	Art Nouveau	RRR
Valter Florence	Animals	*
Wain Louis	Comic	****R
Ward Dudley	Comic	**
Ward Sir Leslie (Spy)	Political cartoons	****R
Weidersheim G.	Children	**
Wennerberg B.	Glamour	***
White Flora	Children	**
Wichera R. R. von	Glamour and children	***
Wielandt M.	Scenic	**
Wimbush H. B.	Scenic	*

Name	Subject	Rarity Factor
Wood Lawson	Comic	**
Woodville R. Caton	Military	****R
Wright Seppings	Shipping	**
Zandrino	Glamour	***

Some of the Internationally known PUBLISHERS of postcards

David Allan & Co.
Alphasa Publishing Co.
Aristophot Co.
Artistic Stationery Co.
Augener Ltd

Bamforth & Co. Ltd
J. Beagles & Co. Ltd
Birn Bros (B.B.)
A. & C. Black
Blum & Degen
Boots Cash Chemists

Cynicus Publishing Co.

Daily Mail, London
Davidson Bros
A. M. Davis
Delittle & Fenwick
E. T. W. Dennis & Sons

Ellis & Wallery Ltd
Max Ettlinger & Co.
Eyre & Spottiswoode

C. W. Faulkner

Frith & Co.

Gale & Polden
W. H. Goss

F. Hartmann
James Henderson
S. Hildesheimer

Inter-Art Co.

Ja-Ja
Jackson & Sons
Jarrolds Ltd
Judges Ltd

Knight Bros

Locomotive Publishing Co
London Stereoscopic Co

Vivian Mansell & Co.
Medici Society
Meissner & Buch
Millar & Lang
Misch & Co.

Nelson & Sons

Ernest Nister
A. Noyer (Paris)

The Philco Publishing Co.
R. P. Phillimore & Co.
Photochrom Co.
Pictorial Stationery Co.
Picture Postcard Co.

Rapid Photo Printing Co.
Regal Art Publishing Co.
Regent Publishing Co.
Rotary Photo Co.
Rotophot
J. W. Ruddock & Sons,
    Lincoln

J. Salmon

E. A. S. Schwerdtfeger & Co.
Stengel & Co.
George Stewart, Edinburgh
Stewart & Woolf
Alfred Stiebel

A. & G. Taylor
Raphael Tuck & Sons Ltd

Valentine & Sons

J. Welch & Sons,
    Portsmouth

Marcus Ward
F. W. Warne & Co.
Wildt & Kray
Woolstone Bros
E. Wrench

Figures 16, 17 and 18 (Pages 200, 201, and 202).
Selected publishers' colophons.

The Regent Publishing Co. Ltd, London

E. A. S. Schwerdtfeger & Co., London

TRADE MARK.

MILTON
Woolstone Bros, London

Photochrom
Co. Ltd,
London and
Tunbridge Wells

Davidson Bros, London
and New York

Taunt & Co., London

Pictorial Stationery Co.,
London

Max Ettlinger & Co. Ltd,
London and New York

American-Souvenir-Card.

American Souvenir Card Co., U.S.A.

C. W. Faulkner & Co. Ltd,
London

Valentine & Sons, Dundee

Raphael Tuck & Sons,
London and New York

Wildt & Kray,
London

Philco Publishing Co.,
London

Millar & Lang, Ltd,
Glasgow and London

F. Hartmann,
Great Britain

Bamforth & Co. Ltd,
England and New York

Misch & Co., Great
Britain

A. &. C. Black, Ltd,
London

The Medici Society,
Ltd, London

Gale & Polden Ltd,
London, Aldershot
and Portsmouth

J. Beagles & Co.,
London

'Boots Cash Chemist',
Nottingham

Birn Bros: (B.B.), London

7 *Some International Postcard Dealers*

Great Britain

John Hall and David MacWilliams, 17 Harrington Road, London S.W.7, England. Classified postcards, Victorian music covers, theatrical figures in Staffordshire china, etc., etc.

Middlesex Collectors Centre, 24 Watford Road, Wembley HA0 3EP, Middlesex, England. Classified postcards, ephemera, etc. Prop: Mr Ken Lawson.

Bath Collectors Centre, 2 Beaufort West, London Road, Bath BA1 6QB, England. Classified postcards, trade cards, cigarette cards, ephemera, coins, etc. Prop: Mr Brian Swallow.

International Postcard Market Ltd, 30 Shirley Avenue, Old Coulsdon, Surrey, England. Classified postcards, trade cards, cigarette cards etc. (postal mailing lists). Prop.: Mr J. H. D. Smith.

Garnet Langton, Burlington Arcade, Bournemouth, Dorset, England.

R.F. Postcards, 17 Hilary Crescent, Rayleigh, Essex, England. Classified postcards, postal history, etc. Prop.: Mrs Joan Venman and Mr Ron Meade.

Lake & Brooks Ltd, 106 Bedford Chambers, Covent Garden, London, England. Postal history and classified postcards. Prop.: Mr Ken Lake and Mr Dave Brooks.

Desmond Chamberlain, P.O. Box 725, London S.W.15, England. Postal history and classified postcards.

Ducal, 5 Weavills Road, Bishopstoke, Eastleigh, Hampshire, England. Classified postcards, military models, etc. Prop.: Mr & Mrs Jack Duke.

Recollections, 2 Monkville Parade, Finchley Road, Temple Fortune, England. Classified postcards. Prop.: Mr Michael Steyn.

J. A. L. Franks Ltd, 140 Fetter Lane, London E.C.4, England. Postal history and classified postcards – ask for Mr Iles.

David Field Ltd, 42 Berkeley Street, Mayfair, London W.1, England. Classified postcards and postal history.

Winchester Stamp Centre, 6b Parchment Street, Winchester, Hampshire, England. Classified postcards and postal history.

Vale, 21 Tranquil Vale, Blackheath, London S.E.3, England. Postal history and classified postcards.

Francis J. Field, Richmond Road, Sutton Coldfield, West Midlands B73 6BJ, England. Aero-philately and aviation postcards.

Burton Collectors Centre, 24 Derby Street, Burton-on-Trent, Staffordshire, England. Classified postcards, Victorian ephemera, etc. Prop.: Mr & Mrs David Matthews.

Pleasures of Past Times, Cecil Court, London, England. Classified postcards and ephemera. Prop.: David Drummond.

Rosina Stevens, 57 Sydenham Rise, London SE23 3XL, England. Classified postcards and ephemera.

Ron. Griffiths, 47 Long Arrotts, Hemel Hempstead, Herts HP1 3EX, England. Postcard sales lists by post only.

Golden Age Postcards, 28 St Peter's Road, Malvern, Worcestershire, England. Postcard sales lists. Prop.: Mr A. Byatt.

Presland Postcards, 3 Beaulieu Court, Basingstoke, Hampshire, England. Classified postcards, postal history etc. Prop.: Mr P. Presland.

H. Richardson, 27B Marchmont Road, Edinburgh, Scotland. Postcard sales lists.

British Auction rooms for postcards

Sotheby's Belgravia, 19 Motcomb Street, London SW1X 8LB, England. Write for catalogues.

Christie's, South Kensington, 85 Old Brompton Road, London SW7 3JS, England. Write for catalogues.

Phillips, 7 Blenheim Street, New Bond Street, London W1 0AS, England. Write for catalogues.

Caxton Hall, Specialized bi-monthly auctions. Write to Mr Ken Lawson, 24 Watford Road, Wembley HA0 3EP, Middlesex, England, for details of catalogues.

France

Write to Joëlle et Gérard Neudin, 35 rue Geoffroy Saint Hilaire, Paris, for information regarding French dealers.

Germany

Write to Willi Bernhard, 2000 Hamburg 73, Wiesenredder 2, West Germany, for information about German dealers.

United States of America

Write to Roy and Marilyn Nuhn, Editors, *The American Postcard Journal*, Box 562, West Haven, Connecticut, U.S.A. for information regarding American dealers.

Bibliography

The following books are recommended for further reading.

The Picture Postcard and its Origins, Frank Staff, Lutterworth Press, U.K., 1966.
Pictures in the Post, Richard Carline, Gordon Fraser, U.K., 1971.
Picture Postcards of the Golden Age, Tonie and Valmai Holt, MacGibbon & Kee, U.K., 1971.
Discovering Picture Postcards, C. W. Hill, Shire Publications, U.K., 1970.
L'Aéronautique a la Belle Époque, George Naudet, Belgium, 1976.
Fantasy Postcards, William Ouellette and Barbara Jones, U.S.A., 1975.
Picture Postcards, Marian Klamkin, David & Charles, U.K., 1974.
French Undressing, Paul Hammond, Jupiter Books, U.K., 1976.
Pioneer Postcards, J. R. Burdick, Nostalgia Press, U.S.A., 1956.
The Comic Postcard in English Life, F. Alderson, David & Charles, U.K., 1969.
With Love – The Erotic Postcard, Erik Norgaard, MacGibbon & Lee, U.K., 1969.
Mucha, Jiri Mucha, Marina Henderson, Aaron Scharf, Academy Editions, U.K., 1974.
The History of the Christmas Card, George Buday, Rockcliff, U.K., 1954.
La Carte Postale Illustrée, Georges Guyonnet, France, 1947.

American Guide to Tuck's, Sally Carver, Carver Cards, U.S.A., 1977

Stevengraphs, Geoffrey Godden, Barrie & Jenkins, U.K., 1971.

Price Guide to Stevengraphs, Austin Sprake, Antique Collectors Club, U.K., 1972.

Book of Bathing Beauties, Ronnie Barker, Hodder & Stoughton, U.K., 1974.

Book of Boudoir Beauties, Ronnie Barker, Hodder & Stoughton, U.K., 1976.

Sauce!, by Ronnie Barker, Hodder & Stoughton, U.K., 1978.

Till the Boys Come Home, Tonie and Valmai Holt, MacGibbon & Lee, U.K., 1977.

Erotic Postcards, Barbara Jones and William Ouellette, Macdonald & Jane's, U.K., 1977.

Postcard Priced Catalogues

Pictons Postcard Catalogue, M. R. Hewlett, Picton Print, Chippenham, U.K. Annually.

IPM Catalogue of Picture Postcards, J. H. D. Smith, IPM Ltd., U.K. Bi-Annually.

Cartes Postales, Gérard et Joelle Neudin, Paris, France. Twice yearly.

Willi Bernhard Postcard Catalogues, Hamburg, West Germany.

Librairie Cartophilique, Andre Fidlier, Paris, France.

Postcard Magazines

The American Postcard Journal, Roy and Marilyn Nuhn, Connecticut, U.S.A.

Postcard Collectors' Gazette, edited by David Pearlman, London, U.K.

Postcard Collectors' Guide, A. J. Butland, Swindon, U.K.

Transy News, H. Richardson, Edinburgh, Scotland.

Index